Unit 1

GCSE English and Engl... ...el

C000098092

Communication

Richard Hoyes

Kim Richardson

Consultant   Elizabeth Whittome

www.heinemann.co.uk

✓ Free online support
✓ Useful weblinks
✓ 24 hour online ordering

01865 888058

Heinemann
Inspiring generations

Heinemann Educational Publishers
Halley Court, Jordan Hill, Oxford OX2 8EJ
Part of Harcourt Education

Heinemann is a registered trademark of Harcourt Education Limited

© Harcourt Education 2006

First published 2006

10 09 08 07 06
10 9 8 7 6 5 4 3 2 1

British Library Cataloguing in Publication Data is available
from the British Library on request.

10-digit ISBN: 0 435368 34 6
13-digit ISBN: 978 0 435368 34 0

Copyright notice

All rights reserved. No part of this publication may be reproduced in any form or by any means (including photocopying or storing
it in any medium by electronic means and whether or not transiently or incidentally to some other use of this publication) without
the written permission of the copyright owner, except in accordance with the provisions of the Copyright, Designs and Patents Act
1988 or under the terms of a licence issued by the Copyright Licensing Agency, 90 Tottenham Court Road, London W1T 4LP.
Applications for the copyright owner's written permission should be adressed to the publisher.

Commissioned by Lionel Bolton
Edited by Simon Brand
Designed by Wooden Ark Studio
Produced by Kamae Design

Original illustrations © Harcourt Education Limited, 2006
Illustrated by Ian West
Cover design by Wooden Ark Studio
Printed by Printer Trento Srl
Cover photo: © Getty Images

Picture research by Bea Ray
Permissions research by Jackie Newman

Acknowledgements

The Publishers gratefully acknowledge the following for permission to reproduce copyright material. Whilst every effort has been
made to trace the copyright holders, in cases where this has been unsuccessful or if any have inadvertently been overlooked, the
Publishers will be pleased to make the necessary arrangements at the first opportunity.

screengrab taken from www.makepovertyhistory.org reprinted with permission; extract from 'Mandela addresses Live 8 finale'
from BBC News at bbcnews.co.uk. Reprinted with permission; extract from 'New guidelines for school meals' from BBC News at
bbcnews.co.uk. Reprinted with permission; extracts from www.feedmebetter.com reprinted with permission of Sweet As Candy
Limited; 'So you're an animal lover, are you?' produced by Viva! © Viva! Reprinted with permission; extract from 'The Omega
Wave' from www.bbc.co.uk/science. Reprinted with permission; screengrab from World Health Organisation website. www.who.int;
screengrab 'About Divine' from www.divinechocolate.com. Reprinted with the kind permission of The Day Chocolate Company
www.divinechocolate.com; extract from 'Still Hungry' by Alex Renton, photo by Romas Foord 2005, The Oberserver, Sunday 14th
August, 2005 Copyright © Guardian Newspapers Limited 2005. Reprinted with permission; screengrab from www.thehungersite.
com © GreaterGood Network. Reprinted with permission; 'The Good Old Days' Were they? Really?' By Jack Dawbney, Flipside
Column, The Farnham Herald © Jack Dawbney; extract from http://www.princeofwales.gov.uk/speeches/agriculture_01061999.html
which is from An article by HRH The Prince of Wales titled 'Questions about Genetically Modified Organisms', The Daily Mail, 1st
June, 1999; Calorie Bible Advert. Reprinted with permission of Weight Loss Resources Ltd; Salubalance Advert © Salus. Reprinted
with the kind permission of Salus UK; extract from ANIMAL FARM by George Orwell. Copyright © George Orwell. Reprinted by
permission of Bill Hamilton as the Literary Executor of the Estate of the late Sonia Brownell Orwell and Secker & Warburg, c/o A. M.
Heath; 'Eat to Beat Pain' from YOURS SPECIAL: HEALTH PLUS Nov/Dec 2003. Reprinted with permission of EMAP; screengrabs from
www.myschool.lunch.co.uk reprinted with permission; extract from BOYS ABOUT BOYS by N Fisher. Reprinted with permission
of Piccadilly Press; 'Hit or Myth?' from Daily Express 5th December, 2003. Reprinted with permission of Express Newspapers
Ltd; extract 'Fawcett responds to Michael Buerk' Fawcett News Release 16 August, 2005. Reprinted with the kind permission of
Fawcett Society; 'There is nothing unmanly about tears' by Bruce Anderson, Political Columnist, The Independent, 8th April 2004.
Reprinted with permission of The Independent; 'It's unattractive and undignified' by Terence Blacker, The Independent, 8th April
2004. Reprinted with permission of The Independent; extract adapted from BRINGING THE BEST OUT IN BOYS by Lucinda Neall,
published by Hawthorn Press, reprinted with permission of Hawthorn Press, Stroud, UK 2002; extracts from 'Life is now lived by
women's rules,' says Buerk' by Craig Brown, The Scotsman, 16th August, 2005. Reprinted with permission of The Scotsman; extracts
from WHY MEN DON'T LISTEN AND WOMEN DON'T READ MAPS by A & B Pease. Copyright © A & B Pease. Reprinted with the
kind permission of Dorie Simmonds Literary Agency on behalf of the authors; extract from http://www.channel4.com/science/
microsites/B/battle_sexes/. Reproduced with permission of Channel 4 Learning. Copyright 4Ventures Ltd; 'Death of the Ladette' by
Laura Neill, The Daily Star, 10th September, 2005. Reprinted with permission of Express Newspapers Limited; photograph of Zoe
Ball Reprinted with permission of Southern News & Pictures; extract from THE BOYS ARE BACK IN TOWN by Simon Carr, published
by Hutchinson. Reprinted by permission of The Random House Group Ltd; extract from 'Games for Girls' by Jessica Kiddle, The
Scotsman, 9th March, 2005. Reprinted with permission of the Scotsman; extract from RACE AGAINST TIME by Ellen MacArthur
(Michael Joseph 2005) Copyright © Ellen MacArthur 2005. Reprinted with permission of Penguin Books UK; The benefits of
coeducation by Michael Mavor. Reprinted with the kind permission of the author; extract from 'Girls and Boys together' from
The Times. © Times Newspapers. Reprinted with permission of NI Syndications; Are girls short changed in the co-ed classroom
from www.gsa.uk.com reprinted with permission of Girl's Schools Association; 'What's good about single-sex schools?' from 0–19
Magazine, March 2005 pp 8–9. Reprinted with permission of 0–19; use of leaflet 'BULLYING RUINS LIVES' reprinted with kind
permission of The Mid-counties Co-operative; use of VO5 Texturising Gum advert. Reprinted with the kind permission of Alberto-
Culver

Tel: 01865 888058 www.heinemann.co.uk

This high quality material is endorsed by Edexcel and has been through a rigorous quality assurance programme to ensure that it is
a suitable companion to the specification for both learners and teachers. This does not mean that its contents will be used verbatim
when setting examinations nor is it to be read as being the official specification – a copy of which is available at www.edexcel.org.uk

Contents

Introduction

How this book will help you

This is a brand new book for an exciting new course. This book prepares you for Edexcel's GCSE Unit 1 Communication. This is a compulsory unit, whether you are taking single or dual award, GCSE English or GCSE English Studies.

This book will help you develop your reading and writing skills. It covers reading and writing generally as well as the specifics of reading on-screen and writing using a computer – as this is how you will be completing the Unit 1B assignment. This book also gives you speaking and listening opportunities as well as suggested activities to complete the Unit 1A coursework.

How Unit 1 is structured

Unit 1 is divided into two parts:
- Unit 1A: Speaking and Listening (40% of the Unit)
- Unit 1B: Reading and Writing (60% of the Unit)

Unit 1A

Unit 1A is coursework in which your teacher will submit a mark out of 40 to the Awarding Body, Edexcel, based on the following three activities completed during the course:
1 Drama-focused activity
2 Group discussion and interaction
3 Individual extended contribution

Across the three activities you will cover the following triplets:
- Explain, describe, narrate
- Explore, analyse, imagine
- Discuss, argue, persuade

Unit 1B

Unit 1B is an assessment in controlled conditions and carries a maximum mark of 80. The assignment covers the following areas:
- Reading Media texts
- Writing to argue, persuade, advise
- Reading Non-fiction texts
- Writing to inform, explain, describe

The tasks in the assignment are based on texts that you have studied before sitting the assessment. There is a detailed explanation of how the assessment works on pages 6–8 and 65–8.

The Unit 1 Assessment Objectives

Assessment Objectives are the criteria the Awarding Body uses to assess your capabilities.

Unit 1A has one Assessment Objective (AO1), divided into three parts, which requires you to:

   i Communicate clearly and imaginatively
      Structure and organise talk
      Adapt talk to different situations
      Use standard English appropriately
  ii Participate in discussion by both speaking and listening
      Judge the nature and purposes of contributions and the roles of participants
 iii Adopt roles and communicate with audiences using a range of techniques

Unit 1B has two Assessment Objectives (AO2 and AO3), divided into separate parts, as detailed in the table below:

	Reading: Media texts Writing: Argue, persuade, advise	Reading: Non-fiction texts Writing: Inform, explain, describe
Reading (AO2) ii Distinguish between fact and opinion and evaluate how information is presented	✓	
iii Follow an argument, identifying implications and recognising inconsistencies		✓
iv Select material appropriate to their purpose, collate material from different sources, and make cross-references		✓
v Understand and evaluate how writers use linguistic, structural and presentational devices to achieve their effects and comment on ways language varies and changes	✓	
Writing (AO3) i Communicate clearly and imaginatively, using and adapting forms for different readers and purposes	✓	✓
ii Organise ideas into sentences, paragraphs and whole texts using a variety of linguistic and structural features	✓	✓
iii Use a range of sentence structures effectively with accurate punctuation and spelling	✓	✓

How this book is structured

This book reflects the way the Unit 1B Assignment is structured. As well as providing teaching and activities you will also find:

- Speaking and listening opportunities – help you practise and complete the coursework for Unit 1A
- Assignment tips – give you pieces of assignment advice
- Key points – summarise the main learning points from a section
- Practise IT – give you basic practical computer activities and tips to help with the Unit 1B assignment
- Checklists of learning – summarise all the main learning points
- Sample assignments – give you the opportunity to practise the skills you have learnt in practice assignments
- Communication text types and toolkits – summarise with examples all the main points of six different text types.

My learning

In this section I will:
- *learn how to approach the media section of Unit 1B (pages 8–12)*
- *learn and practise the skills in reading media texts and writing to argue, persuade, advise (pages 9–52)*
- *practise speaking and listening activity for Unit 1A*
- *have a go at a sample assignment, with help from assignment advice (pages 53–60).*

Introduction to media texts

What are media texts?

In the first half of the assignment you will be reading media texts and writing a piece related to them. Media texts could include:

- newspapers
- magazines
- advertisements
- TV
- film
- videos
- websites.

There is more to reading these texts than simply reading the words. Their structure, layout and design are just as important.
Many media texts reach their audience in electronic or digital format through a TV, cinema or computer screen. All the media texts that you will study in Unit 1 are designed to be read on screen, and this makes them different from printed texts: they are designed differently and we read them differently.

Activity 1

The following texts all relate to the film *Supersize Me*, which was about the fast-food industry in America.

1 Sort these texts into two groups: those that are print-based, and those designed to be read on screen.

2 Explain how some of them could exist both on screen and in print.

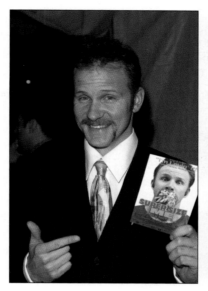 

a) the film *Supersize Me*
b) a novel based on the film
c) a billboard advertisement for the film
d) a report in the *Daily Mirror* about the award won by the film's director, Morgan Spurlock
e) comments on the film in an online chat forum
f) a review of the film in an online edition of *The Times* newspaper
g) a TV documentary about the making of the film
h) a DVD version of the film
i) the official website for the film
j) an extract from the screenplay (the script) of the film, as part of an educational CD-ROM.

The reading skills you will be assessed on

For your assignment, you will be given a series of media texts to read, all related to a particular theme. When answering questions about these texts, you need to show:

- that you understand what they are saying
- that you understand how and why they are written in the way they are
- that you can comment about them and have your own opinions about them.

The diagram below describes the reading skills that will be assessed in the assignment. On the left are the examiner's words; on the right that information is explained in more detail.

'You will be assessed on your ability to distinguish between fact and opinion and evaluate how information is presented.'	You need to show that you understand the style, structure and presentation of a range of media texts. This means understanding the content of the texts, and commenting on how well that information is presented (including visual presentation), taking the audience and purpose of the texts into account. Some of the content will be facts, and some will be opinions. You need to be able to tell the difference and know how/why they are used.
'You will be assessed on your ability to understand and evaluate how writers use linguistic, structural and presentational devices to achieve their effects, and comment on the way language varies and changes.'	This is all about how words, structure and presentation are used to get the message across. Again, you need to think about this in the context of purpose and audience. It's even better if you can think more widely about how the media texts reflect the society that creates them. To get the very best marks in this exam you will need to show you can appreciate how texts engage our feelings and how they alter our way of seeing things.

You may also be asked in the assignment to compare two media texts. When you do this, you will have to make clear and effective references to the texts.

The writing skills you will be assessed on

In the media section, you will also be given a writing task. This will relate in some way to the texts that you have been studying. You will be assessed on how well you can write to **argue**, to **persuade** and to **advise**. Usually, the writing task will combine these purposes in one piece of writing.

The diagram below describes what writing skills will be assessed in the assignment. On the left are the examiner's words; on the right that information is explained in more detail.

'You will be assessed on your ability to communicate clearly and imaginatively, using and adapting forms for different readers and purposes.'	• You have to express yourself clearly, but you also have to use words and ideas in a varied, effective and imaginative way. The exam will give you a situation to write in and a target audience to write for. The writing could take a variety of forms – it might be a letter or a speech, for example. • You will need to bear your readers or listeners clearly in mind at all times.
'You will be assessed on your ability to organise ideas into sentences, paragraphs and whole texts using a variety of linguistic and structural features.'	• You will need to structure your text effectively so that the piece 'hangs together'. That includes beginning and ending well, organising points in paragraphs, and using presentational devices such as bullet points, if appropriate. • Your sentences need to work together well.
'You will be assessed on your ability to use a range of sentence structures effectively with accurate punctuation and spelling.'	• You need to show that you can craft sentences in varied and effective ways, by writing sentences of different kinds and different lengths. Do you need a short snappy sentence, for example? Or a longer, more descriptive or explanatory one? • Marks are also awarded for correct grammar, punctuation and spelling.

Sample assignment on media texts

To help you understand what this section is leading up to this is what the first half of your assignment paper will look like. You should not tackle this assignment now as the full assignment, together with the texts, is given at the end of the Media section (page 58). By the time you have studied this section in detail you will be ready to do the full assignment.

Remember

- You have 4 hours in total to complete all the tasks in the assignment. That includes the second half of the paper, on Non-fiction texts. So the Media questions should take approximately half that time.
- Note that the topics for the Media and Non-fiction texts are different in this book. In the actual Edexcel assessment the topic is the same for the Media and Non-fiction texts.
- In your actual assignment you will already have been studying the texts in the classroom for a few weeks before you are given the assignment.

The annotations show you what skills you need to learn, and where this book will help you to practise them.

> You need to be able to time yourself in the assignment room. 'Assignment tips' throughout the book give you practical help on how to tackle the assignment.

> You need to be able to key in your final draft on a computer. 'Practise IT' boxes throughout the book give you practical help on how to improve your keying-in skills.

> You need to be able to analyse and compare media texts, commenting on how effectively they have been written and presented for their purpose. (See page 19.)

> You need to know the features and style of a letter.

> You need to be able to write effectively to these three different purposes. The letter will explain/argue (see pages 34–43 for writing to argue), persuade parents (see pages 44–50 for writing to persuade) and give advice (see pages 51–56 for writing to advise).

HEALTHY EATING FOR SCHOOLS

You have a maximum of 4 hours to complete all the tasks below and on page 110.

You must study the following media texts in order to complete this task.

1 Three pages from the celebrity chef Jamie Oliver's Feed Me Better website:
- home page
- Why Feed Me Better?
- Manifesto for Change.

2 One page from the World Health Organisation website.

3 Two pages from the website My School Lunch:
- home page
- 'Why should I choose a school lunch for my child?'

Stage 1: Analysing the texts

You are a member of the school council. You have been asked to investigate designing a website for the school council, which would cover concerns of students, such as school dinners. You have been given some media texts to look at.

Task 1

Write a review of the websites, identifying the techniques that they use to achieve their aims. Your review will help your school council make its own website effective.

You must study the websites listed above in order to write you review.

For your review you must select **only two** of these websites.

In your review you should compare the material from your two websites by:
- identifying the techniques that are being used to encourage healthy eating
- commenting on the visual/design techniques
- commenting on the language used in your chosen websites.

You must refer closely to the **two** websites throughout and must include examples from these websites in order to illustrate the points that you are making.

In this task you will be assessed on your reading skills.

(20 marks for Reading)

Task 2

Your school has now adopted a healthy eating policy, which it is promoting on the new school council website. Write a letter from the school council to parents persuading them:
- to let their children have school dinners
- that the healthy eating policy might be put into practice at home.

Support your points with material from ANY of the websites provided and anything else you know about healthy eating.

You will be assessed for your skills in writing to **argue**, **persuade** and **advise**.

(20 marks for Writing)

A Reading media texts

Understanding structure

> ### My learning
>
> In 'Understanding structure' I will:
> * investigate how structure is an important aspect of a text
> * learn how an on-screen text is structured
> * think about how the structure of media texts allows the audience to interact with them.

Putting texts together

Structure is about how a text is put together. Texts are structured differently depending on their form and purpose.

> ### Activity 1
>
> With a partner, think about the types of television programme listed below.
> a) a documentary
> b) an advert
> c) a sitcom series
> d) Saturday afternoon sports coverage
> e) the main evening news
>
> What is important about the structure of each one? Write down some ideas in note form, and be prepared to share them in a class discussion. Think about questions such as:
> * How long is the programme.
> * Is the presenter on screen all the time.
> * Are there short bursts of material loosely tied together?
> * Or is it a slower, more careful, approach?
> * Is the programme spread over several weeks?

Websites are structured in a particular way. Look at this typical web page, which comes from the Make Poverty History website.

3 This is the title of this web page. Why are the titles of the other web pages repeated on the top navigation bar?

4 This is the link to the site's home page. What is a home page? Does it matter that the term 'home page' (or 'home') does not actually appear on this page?

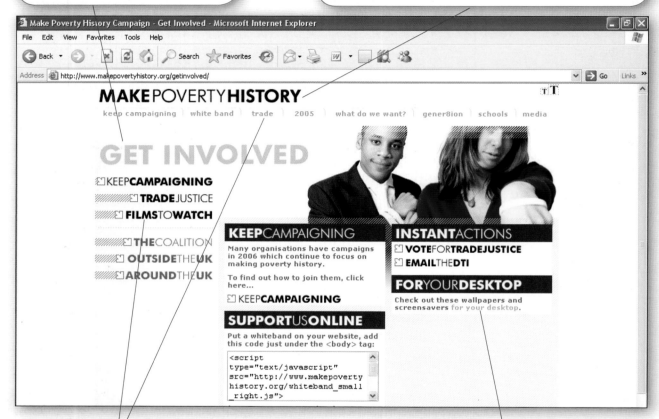

1 These are called navigation bars. Why do you think they are given that name? What do they do? How do they affect how you read the page?

2 The text highlighted in orange is a hyperlink. It links the reader to pages both inside the Make Poverty History website and outside. How does this affect the way you read the website? (Compare it with how you would read a book.)

Activity 2

Some of the features of this web page are annotated. Answer the questions in these boxes.

Reading the text

We will now focus on how the text (as words) is put together on the page. This is another aspect of the structure of media texts.

Activity 3

A student commenting on the Make Poverty History web page says the following:

> There are a lot of boxes, and each box tells us about – or tells us to do – something different. The headings in capitals show the reader where each block of text begins. There are not that many words in each box, and there are not that many words on the page overall.

Assignment tip

When you compare texts in the assignment, always refer to the audience and purpose of each one. Key differences between texts can often be explained in part by thinking about them in the context of their audience and purpose.

1 Look at the web page from the World Health Organization (below). Comment in a similar way to the student above about how the WHO text is structured. Look at the quantity of text on the page and what its purpose is.

2 Write a comment explaining why the two web pages you have studied have different ways of presenting their text. You will need to think about the audience and purpose of each text.

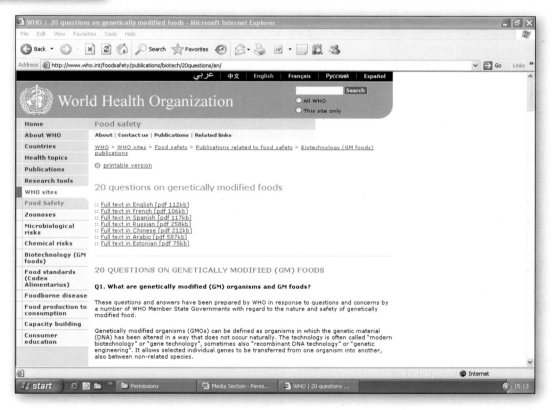

Reading news stories

The structure of news stories is the same, whether the news is on screen or in print. The key facts are given first, often answering the questions Who?, What?, Why?, When? and Where? The writer then gives further detail, which fills in the background.

Mandela addresses Live 8 finale

Nelson Mandela addressed the crown in a recorded message

An international line-up of stars joined the call to eradicate poverty at Edinburgh's climactic Live 8 concert, which was addressed by Nelson Mandela.

Almost 60,000 music fans gathered at Murrayfield Stadium for the Live 8 The Final Push gig, as G8 leaders arrived for talks in Gleneagles.

In a recorded message, the former South African president said: "Let's work to make poverty history this year".

The concert ended with a rousing performance by soul legend James Brown.

In his message, which was introduced by U2 frontman Bono, Mandela said: "Sometimes it falls upon a generation to be great. You can be that generation. You have that opportunity."

The former South African president said: "Let's work to make poverty history this year. Then we can all stand with our heads held high."

Bono said millions supported the campaign to end poverty

Jazz pianist Jamie Cullum sang the Beatles classic, *All You Need Is Love*, with Natasha Bedingfield, who also sang her hit *These Words*.

Scottish favourites Wet Wet Wet performed another Beatles song, *With A Little Help From My Friends* and their biggest hit, *Love Is All Around*.

Pop band McFly were followed by Big Brother presenter Davina McCall who came on stage accompanied by a delegation of children from C8, the children's version of G8, which began on Sunday.

She said: 'In Africa every single minute 20 children die needAlessly just because they were born poor. It can be stopped.'

Girl group Sugababes were followed on stage by U2 star Bono who delivered a message to the G8 leaders.

He said that he had been to Gleneagles and given G8 leaders permission to spend money 'ending extreme poverty in our lifetime'.

from BBC News at bbcnews.co.uk

Activity 4

1 Why are the key facts of a news story given first? What does this tell us about how we read newspapers and news sites?

2 Read 'Mandela addresses Live 8 finale' from the BBC news website again. Where does the first section end? How has it answered each of the five 'W' questions listed above?

3 If you have access to the Internet, find three news stories. Work out where the 'key facts' section of the story ends in each case.

Understanding news values

How do newspaper editors and TV news programme editors decide which stories are run first? Why are some stories headline news and some not? Such decisions determine the overall structure of the newspaper or programme.

Below are some of the criteria for what makes a newsworthy story.
- **Celebrity status:** it mentions important people, names we recognise.
- **Now factor:** it is of topical importance – it is happening *now*.
- **Clarity**: its meaning and message are clear and definite.
- **Size**: it involves a lot of people.

- **Human interest**: it is about people rather than issues in the abstract sense.
- **Bad news is newsworthy**: if a story has a bad side to it, or sounds alarming, then it is probably good for a newspaper or bulletin.

Activity 5

Re-read the G8 concert story (see page 12) and see if the above criteria apply to it. Arrange your ideas in a table like the one below, filling in the gaps. Can you think of any other news values that are missing from this list?

Celebrity status	Now factor	Clarity	Size	Human interest	Bad news is newsworthy	Other?
Nelson Mandela, world-famous statesman, speaks …					20 children per minute die needlessly in Africa	

Interactive texts

Media texts are often interactive. This means that they are structured in such a way that the audience can have an effect on the text, as well as the text having an effect on the audience.

Key points

- You need to be able to comment on how media texts are structured.
- Structure includes how the texts are put together and the way the words are positioned on the page.
- Texts are structured differently depending on audience and purpose.
- Some media texts are structured to allow the audience to interact with them.

Activity 6

Look again at the Make Poverty History web page on page 10. Jot down answers to the following questions.

1 What activities are suggested that people can do?

2 The website urges people to contact their member of parliament:

When thousands and thousands of people send a well-timed text, a short email, or leave a phone message, change begins to take place. We're creating a virtual army of people prepared to give a couple of minutes per week to save real lives.

a) What three methods of communication are mentioned here?
b) What might be the advantages of each one?
c) The last sentence says that the campaign is creating a virtual army to save real lives. In what way does the website audience make a virtual army? Think about the possible meanings of the word 'virtual' here.
d) What is the effect of the contrast between 'virtual' and 'real' in 'to save real lives'?

Understanding language

My learning

In 'Understanding language' I will:
- *distinguish facts from opinions, and learn how they can influence an audience*
- *explore how language can be used to persuade, including emotive language*
- *compare the use of formal and informal language in three media texts.*

The language of media texts varies hugely, depending on the nature of the text, its purpose and its audience. One text may be a pop-up selling a holiday; another may be informing a specialist audience about some scientific research findings.

Identifying facts and opinions

A FACT is a piece of knowledge or information that can be proved to be true:
e.g. *Paris is the capital of France.*

An OPINION is a person's own view about something:
e.g. *Paris is the liveliest capital city in Europe.*

Some words can give you a clue that a sentence contains an opinion:
- words like 'should', 'ought', 'must', which often give someone's view, e.g. 'You must eat healthily'
- adjectives, which describe what one person thinks about something, e.g. 'The soup looks appetising'.

Activity 7

1 Identify which of the following are facts and which are opinions.

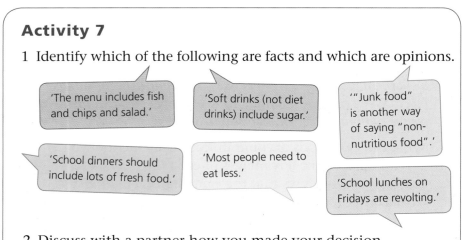

'The menu includes fish and chips and salad.'

'Soft drinks (not diet drinks) include sugar.'

'"Junk food" is another way of saying "non-nutritious food".'

'School dinners should include lots of fresh food.'

'Most people need to eat less.'

'School lunches on Fridays are revolting.'

2 Discuss with a partner how you made your decision.

Thinking about purpose

You would expect information-based texts to contain more facts.

Practise IT

Bullet points
When creating lists it is often useful to use bullet points to make them stand out from other text. To use bullet points you can click on Format at the top of the screen and select Bullets and Numbering. Then you can select the style of bullet point you wish to use.

Activity 8

Read the extract below from the BBC online news, then complete these tasks and questions.

1 List three facts from the first three paragraphs of the extract.

2 The fourth paragraph refers to an opinion. What opinion?

3 If this paragraph had said 'We need to consult the food industry, schools and nutritionists, as school menus are unhealthy', how would that alter the purpose of the text?

4 Where else is an opinion given? What method does the writer use to show the reader that this isn't the BBC's opinion?

5 What other media texts are mainly factual? To answer this question you will need to think about their purpose and audience.

New guidelines for school meals

Parents are to get more say on the quality of school food

New guidelines on the nutritional value of processed foods such as beefburgers and sausages will be introduced into schools in England from September.

Education Secretary Ruth Kelly is to reveal plans to tighten the health requirements for school meals.

Parents will get more say on the quality of the food, she will reveal.

The food industry, schools and nutritionists will also be consulted on what should be on menus, which have been criticised as 'unhealthy'.

'It is important that parents have confidence in what goes on in the school kitchen,' Ms Kelly told the BBC.

from BBC News at bbcnews.co.uk.

15

Mixing fact and opinion

Media texts often combine facts and opinions. One important skill is learning to tell the difference between what is fact and what is opinion.

Read the extract below from the home page of Feed Me Better (FMB), the website promoting chef Jamie Oliver's campaign to improve school meals. The sentence 'The campaign became front page news' could mean either or both of the following.

- It appeared on the front pages of some newspapers.
- It is very important news (front page news is often sensational and amazing).

So the sentence has both a fact and an opinion in it.

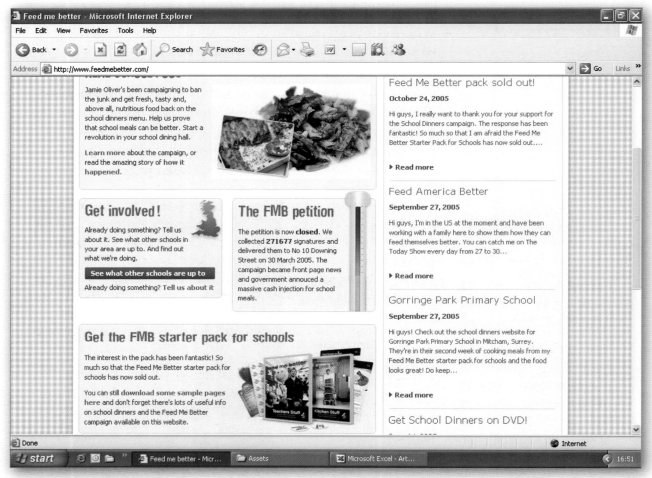

Copyright © Jamie Oliver 2006

Activity 9

Look at the extract opposite, then complete the tasks and questions below.

1 Draw up a table of facts and opinions included in the webpage, like the one started below. In the third column, say why you think the quotations you have chosen for the second column are opinions.

Facts	Opinions	Reason
'There were 271677 signatures'	Interest in the pack has been fantastic	What does 'fantastic' mean? One person's 'fantastic' might be quite different to anothers!

2 'The government announced a massive cash injection for schools.'
   a) What is the fact included in this sentence?
   b) How has the writer used language to express an opinion?
   c) Comment on how effective this is.

3 Facts can be used in particular ways to create an effect. For example, the statement about the petition is followed immediately by the statement about front page news and government money.
   a) What does this imply about the effect of the petition?
   b) What else could have caused the campaign to be front page news? What else could have caused the government to provide extra money for school meals?
   c) Look at the section about the FMB starter pack. What else could have caused the pack to run out? (Think about the number that may have been produced.) As a reader of media texts, you should practise questioning facts as well as opinions.

4 This extract comes from the home page of Jamie Oliver's campaign website. What purpose(s) do you think the home page has? How does this explain the mixture of facts and opinions that you have identified?

Practise IT

Tables
In the assignment, you may want to keep notes on the computer in the form of a table. Remind yourself how to create a table: go to the Toolbar at the top of the screen; click on Table then Insert, then select Table. Draw up a simple table of 'Junk food' and 'Healthy food'. Make these two phrases the headings for your columns.

Using language to persuade

Many media texts are designed to persuade the audience to do something, buy something or agree with some idea. Writers of texts like this use language in particular ways, including:

- using powerful verbs and adjectives to engage the reader's interest and feelings
- asking questions, to get the reader on their side
- repetition and other sound effects (e.g. alliteration), to make an impact
- using first- and second-person pronouns (*I/me*, *you*, *we/us*) to make the text personal
- including commands that tell the reader to do something.

Activity 10

Read the extract on page 19, which comes from another part of the Feed Me Better website. It is part of Jamie Oliver's 'Manifesto for change'.

1 'Teach' is a powerful verb and 'varied' is a powerful adjective. Find another example of both a powerful verb and adjective in the extract. Say why each is effective.

2 Where does the writer ask a question? What is the purpose of the question here?

3 'Put cookery back on the curriculum' (section 4) uses alliteration (the repitition of the same consonant sound). Find another example of alliteration in the extract. Why do you think the writer has used this technique?

4 Where are words repeated to make a point?

5 Where does the writer directly address the reader? How effective is this?

6 Explain why you would expect to find persuasive techniques like these in a 'manifesto'. (A manifesto is a statement of intentions, usually made by a political party.)

7 Which of the following audiences do you think the manifesto is aimed at? Explain what the manifesto is trying to get these audiences to do, think or feel.
   a) schoolchildren
   b) people interested in helping with Jamie's campaign
   c) people who like watching Jamie Oliver on TV
   d) the government department in charge of school meals
   e) school dinner ladies.

Assignment tip

Skimming is used to give you a quick overall sense of the meaning of a text.
Scanning is used to find specific bits of information in a text.
For both techniques you should:
- read it quickly
- try not to read every word
- use clues like titles and illustrations

Assignment tip

In the assignment you will often have to return to texts you have been studying, to check what information or features they contain, or to find a quotation to use. Don't rely on your memory, but use your skills of skimming and scanning to find the information you need.

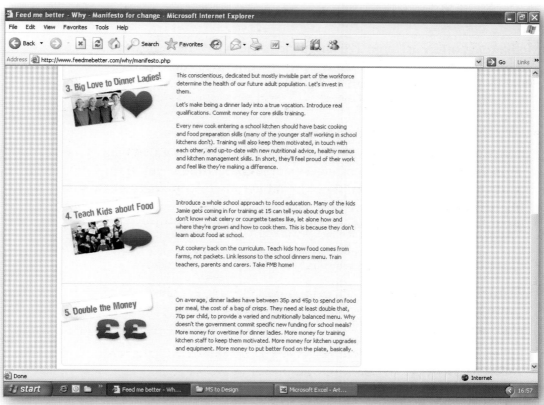

Copyright © Jamie Oliver 2006

Speaking and listening

Speaking and listening opportunity

AO1(iii) *Adopt roles and communicate with audiences using a range of techniques*
This is a ***drama-focused*** activity. It will be used to assess how well you can ***explore/analyse/imagine***.

In groups of five, act out a mock radio discussion about junk food. Use the roles of a celebrity chef, a school dinner lady, a government health spokesperson, the manager of a fast food restaurant, the chairperson.

1 Choose your role. Discuss with a partner in your group what you think your attitude to junk food will be in the radio discussion. Make notes.
2 Practise discussing in role before you go 'on air'.
3 Perform your discussion. You will be responding to questions from the studio audience (the class).

To gain good marks you need to:
– *keep a role going effectively, engaging the audience's interest*
– *use different dramatic techniques to do this*
– *show that you really understand the issues behind the role-play*
– *show that you have some good ideas, and that you can use drama to communicate them.*

Identifying emotive language

Media texts often use emotive language to help get their message across. Emotive language is words, phrases and ideas designed to provoke strong feelings in an audience.

Activity 11

Look at the advert below. It is included on the website of Viva!, a pressure group that encourages people to become vegetarian and vegan. Copy and complete the table to help you analyse the writer's use of emotive language.

Word/phrase/idea	What it makes you feel	How effective it is
'So you're an animal lover, are you?'	'animal lover' appeals to the good side of you	Effective, because it gets you on their side, and draws you in
'about a billion … that could do with your help'	There are a lot of needy animals – and I can help them	
'They can all feel pain, misery and despair'		
'there are few laws to protect them'	Animals are unprotected – victims	
'where most pigs are imprisoned'		
'to give birth and feed their young'	Think about piglets and other baby animals, and how they are born into terrible conditions	

So you're an animal lover, are you?

If so, there are about a billion in the UK that could do with your help. That's how many are killed for meat every year and most are factory farmed. They can all feel pain, misery and despair yet there are few laws to protect them.

Viva!

For a free information pack call Viva! now: 0117 944 1000
www.factoryfarming.org.uk www.viva.org.uk

The farrowing crate. Impossible even to turn around but where most pigs are imprisoned to give birth and feed their young

Produced by Viva! at www.viva.org.uk

Formal and informal

To understand how far language, whether spoken or written, is formal or informal you need to consider the purpose, audience and context of the language use. In the first example below, the purpose is to get the job; the audience is likely to be a manager and the context is a job interview.

Here are some simple examples of formal and informal language use.

1 The spoken language used during a job interview tends to be more formal than informal.
2 The written language used in reports tends to be more formal than informal.
3 The spoken language used between friends is likely to be more informal than formal.
4 The written language used in an email between friends is likely to be more informal than formal.

However, in all of the examples above there are likely to be exceptions. For instance, in the job interview example if the person being interviewed said "I'm wicked at typing" this would be considered by most to be informal (and an unwise thing to say!).

Discuss any other exceptions you can think of for the above four examples.

Assignment Tip

In your assignment you will need to refer to features of the texts to support your view. Pick the most relevant features, and make sure you quote them accurately, using inverted commas to show quoted material.

Practise IT

Headings
When writing a report you will often need to use headings to highlight different sections of text. To do this you will need to leave appropriate line spaces either side of your heading using the Return key. To make the heading stand out put the text in Bold by clicking the Bold button and make it bigger by selecting a higher number in the Font Size drop down box, 18 to 20 is about right.

Activity 12

Read the three texts that follow on pages 22–23.

1 Working in pairs, scan each text for examples of formal and informal language. Draw up a table to show your results.

2 On your own, write a short report comparing the texts. Follow this plan:

1st paragraph	Introduce your report, e.g. 'I am going to compare the use of formal and informal language …'. Include a definition of any terms you use.
2nd paragraph	Analyse the use of language in Text 1. Remember to quote examples from the text to back up your view.
3rd paragraph	Repeat for Text 2.
4th paragraph	Repeat for Text 3.
5th paragraph	Conclusion. Relate your findings to the purpose and audience of each text.

Text 1 is taken from Jamie Oliver's Feed Me Better campaign website.

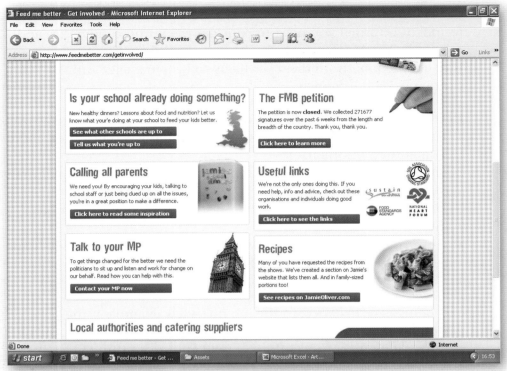

Copyright © Jamie Oliver 2006

Text 2 is taken from the 'Science and Nature' page on the BBC's website.

Science and Nature Human Body & mind

The Omega wave

Fish oils are supposed to boost our brainpower. But do the facts really stack up? We went in search of the evidence.

Elliot is nine years old. A year ago, he was falling behind in his schoolwork, particularly reading – which he found a struggle. He had little interest in studying and would crash on the sofa to watch TV when he got home from school.

But over the past year, a dramatic change has taken place in Elliot. He has soared through the Harry Potter books and now heads to the library after the school bell has sounded.

Elliot has been taking part in a scientific study on more than 100 children from 12 Durham schools. The children were required to take a course of capsules with their meals for the duration of six months.

'His reading jumped 18 months [over the trial period]. He's just a lot more interested in everything. He's even developed an interest in classical music,' says Sheila, Elliot's mother.

Problems vanished

Over the course of the year, Elliot's academic problems disappeared.

Mark, 10, who is in the year above Elliot at Timothy Hackworth School in Shildon, Durham, experienced similar changes.

from BBC website bbc.co.uk/science.

Text 3 is taken from the World Health Organization website.

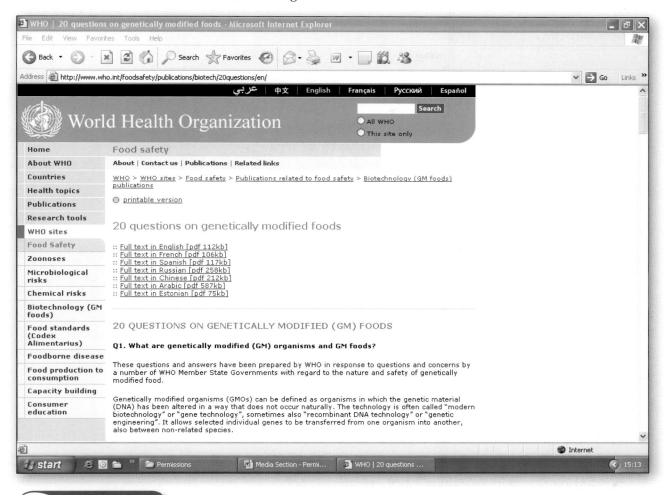

Key points

- Facts and opinions can both be used to influence an audience.
- Key ingredients of persuasive language include powerful verbs and adjectives, questions, repetition and other sound effects, first- and second-person pronouns and commands.
- Media texts often use emotive language to help get their message across.
- The formality of language in media texts varies according to audience and purpose.

Understanding presentation

My learning

In 'Understanding presentation' I will:
- learn about how important the visual aspect of media texts is
- investigate what devices are used to present words, images and overall design
- explore how different images are used for different purposes
- compare the presentational devices used in different texts.

Media texts rely on appearance far more than print-based texts, so when we read them, we are reading a lot of presentational devices as well as a lot of words.

Investigating presentational devices

'Presentational devices' means the features that relate to a text's visual appearance. They include:
- **presentation of words** – headings, subheadings, font used, colour and size, bold, italic and underlining
- **illustrations** – logos, photos, graphics
- **overall design** – how all of the above 'work together' to create an effect.

Activity 13

Look at the 'About Divine' page from the website of Divine, a fair-trade chocolate brand (see page 25). Some of the presentational features are labelled. Read the labels and answer the questions.

Then discuss which of the presentational features overall are:
- most effective and why
- least effectivce and why

1 This is the company **logo** – an image which identifies it. What does this logo suggest?

2 This is the company **slogan**. How does it work together with the logo?

3 The **design** uses hearts in the hyperlink here. Where else are hearts used on the page, and why?

4 This **photo** shows cocoa beans. Why has it been chosen? Explain why the two other main photos have been chosen, and what effect they have.

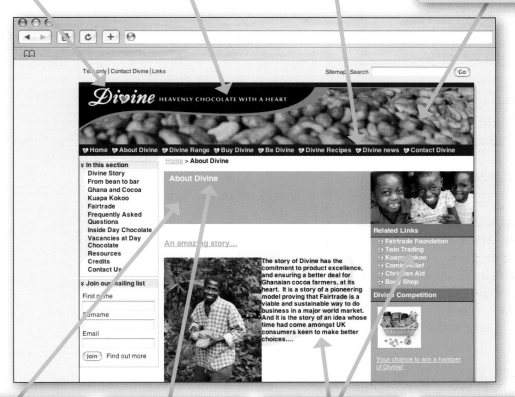

5 Dark orange is the main **colour** used on the page. Why? Is it effective?

6 This is the **title** of the page. How do we know? What other methods are used to show headings and subheadings?

7 The same **font** is used throughout, but varied by the use of bold, underline and white-out. Find an example of each and say whether it is effective.

8 What do you think of the **design** overall? Does everything work together well? Is it distinctive?

Different pictures for different purposes

When you assess the presentational devices used in media texts, you need to look closely at the images used. You should ask not just 'How many illustrations?' but 'What kind of illustrations?'. Images, like words, are carefully chosen for maximum effect.

Activity 14

1 Look at the images of food shown opposite in Text 1 and Text 2. The first is a hard-hitting magazine article on what the world's children are having for supper tonight. The second comes from a government website giving guidance to school caterers on the kinds of meals they should be providing.

2 What is the purpose of each image? Read the following and decide on the most appropriate statement:

Text 1
- To make me want to give money to countries in need.
- To make me grateful for what I've got and glad I don't live there.
- To show the harsh contrast between developed and less developed countries.
- To inform me, so I know what's going on in the world.

Text 2
- To show caterers exactly what should go in the meals they cook
- To show what in general, makes up a healthy diet.
- To illustrate in a colourful way the introductory page of the website
- To give caterers an idea of the sorts of meals they could produce.

3 Write two or three paragraphs summarizing what you can see in the two images. You might want to focus on the following.
- Colour
- Style
- Content
- Size
- How the picture relates to the text.
  How far is each image effective for its purpose?
  Give your reasons.

Practise IT

Paragraphing
In your assignment you will have to make use of a lot of paragraphs. You need to leave appropriate line spaces between the paragraphs. You can do this by pressing the Return key twice. However, you should not indent the start of the next paragraph as you would when writing by hand, instead the writing should begin at the very start of the line.

Text 1 (below) is taken from the Observer Food Monthly supplement.

Still hungry

The world produces more than enough food for all of us. So why will 200 million children go to sleep tonight hungry? Alex Renton investigates the relationship between food and poverty – and what a child calls supper around the world

For supper tonight, three-quarters of us will be eating mainly stodge – a pile of carbohydrates. One in 10 people on the planet will dine on a mash of cassava root (remember tapioca?), much of Africa will eat starchy porridges of plantain, yam, maize or other grains. Across the tropics, the evening meal will be based on boiled rice – the staple food of a third of all humanity. It's not very Atkins, but it is good, useful food: a solid belly filler, as anyone who's eaten African fufu or ugali will tell you.

© Romas Foord 2005

Observer Food Monthly, Sunday 14 August 2005

Text 2 comes from a government website.

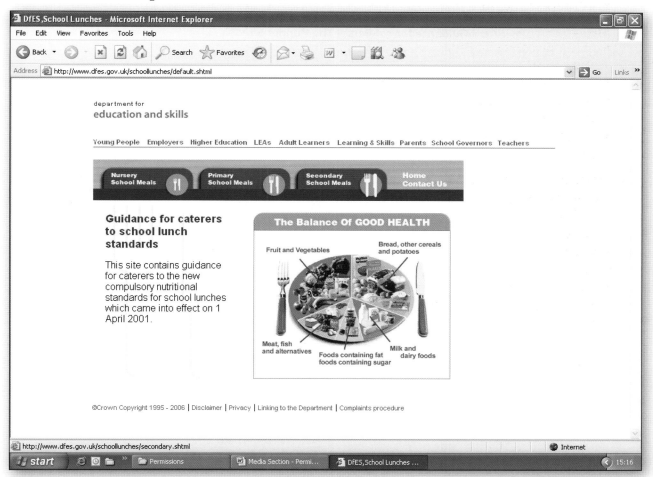

www.dfes.gov.uk © Crown Copyright

Comparing media texts

When you compare the presentation of media texts, you need to do it in a careful, logical and well-ordered way.

Activity 15

You have looked carefully at the image in the government website in Text 2 (page 27). Now you are going to compare the overall presentation of the web page with that of the Hunger Site (see page 29). This is an American site selling goods made in the developing world, alongside making appeals for donations to ease world hunger.

1 Draw up a table like the one started below to record the different presentational features and their effects. Briefly describe the content and give your opinion about how effective each feature is.

	Guidance for caterers	**The Hunger Site**
Purpose of text		
Audience of text	School caterers.	
Presentation of words: • headings/subheadings • size, style and colour.		Subheadings in capitals, which helps make them stand out.
Images: • logos and slogans • photographs • graphics.		Lots of small images – shows how many different charities there are to support.
Overall design: • use of colour • how well does it work altogether? • is it distinctive?	The links in the navigation bar are designed like dividers in a folder – very suitable for a text aimed at schools.	

2 Write up your notes into three or four paragraphs comparing these two texts. Follow the same organisation you have used in the table, but write in sentences and paragraphs.

Assignment tip

When you get your assignment materials, record the purpose and audience of each one in a table like the one on this page, then record all the presentational features and their effects. Although you will not be able to take this table (or any notes) into the assignment room, it will focus your thinking and act as a good revision guide. It should help you to answer any question set on the texts.

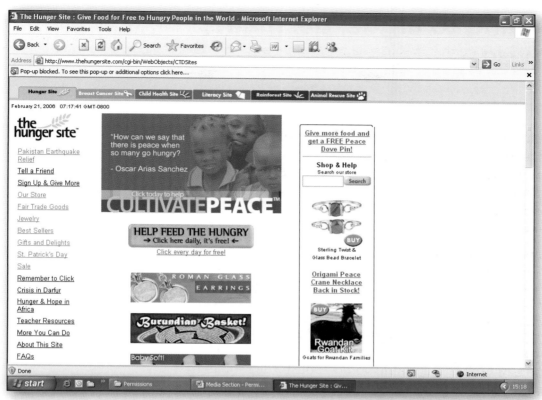

© *GreaterGood Network.*

Key points

- Media texts rely on visual appearance far more than print-based texts.
- Images, like words, are carefully chosen for maximum effect.
- Presentational devices include the way words are presented (headings, style and size of font, use of bold, etc.), the illustrations (photos, graphics) and the overall design, including colour.
- When you compare the presentational devices used in media texts you must be as careful and logical as when you compare their words.

Speaking and listening

Speaking and listening opportunity

AO1(i) *Communicate clearly and imaginatively, structuring and organising your talk and using Standard English appropriately*
This is an *individual speaking* activity. It will be used to assess how well you can *explain/describe/narrate*.

Imagine that intelligent life on another planet has access to the Earth's Internet, but is not able to speak to its people. Through exploring the Internet, therefore, aliens can draw conclusions about the nature of humans.

Choose any one of the websites discussed so far in this book. Give a talk to your class, explaining what conclusions the aliens might draw from it about life on Earth.

To gain good marks you need to:
- *speak confidently and fluently*
- *adapt the style of your talk to the needs of your audience*
- *show that you really understand the subject matter*
- *speak in Standard English, using a range of vocabulary and grammatical structures*
- *respond to questions or comments in an appropriate way.*

B Writing to argue, persuade, advise

Writing to argue

My learning

In 'Writing to argue' I will:
- learn about the key features of writing to argue
- write argument texts, thinking about structure, content, tone and style
- explore the special techniques that argument texts use
- take account of audience and purpose in my writing.

When you write to argue, you need to present and develop a particular point of view, with the aim of persuading people to agree with you, or at least appreciate the points you are making. Argument texts range from a letter to the manager of a shop arguing why you should be given a refund for faulty goods, to a lengthy article in a newspaper arguing that Britain should abolish the monarchy.

Activity 16

Here are some points made by students about fast food.
- 'Fast food, so-called junk food, is fine in moderation, as part of a balanced diet.'
- 'It is quick, cheap and convenient.'
- 'There is no "snobby" side to fast food, unlike "posh" restaurants. All kinds of people eat there and are welcome.'

These are obviously points made by people who are defending fast food.

Working in pairs, draw up a list of bad points about fast food.

Building an argument

The *Oxford English Dictionary* defines argument as 'a process of reasoning'. All the points listed in Activity 1 are simple statements of opinion. To turn them into an argument, they need to become part of a process of reasoning. This means adding two key features.
- A statement of your conclusion (what you are trying to prove). Note that your conclusion doesn't have to come at the end of your argument – it's a different kind of conclusion.
- Some 'glue' to bind your list of points together. This means joining up your thinking and using connectives to show where your argument is going.

Activity 17

The points in favour of fast food have been turned into a short argument (below).

1 Discuss with a partner:
   a) where this argument includes the two key features of argument texts
   b) how these features make it a more effective piece of writing.

I do not believe that we should avoid fast food restaurants at all costs. Fast food, so-called junk food, is fine in moderation, as part of a balanced diet. It is also quick and convenient. Furthermore, all kinds of people eat in fast food restaurants and are welcome there, because there is no 'snobby' side to fast food, unlike 'posh' restaurants.

2 On your own, turn your list of points against fast food into a proper argument. Remember to state your conclusion somewhere (the beginning or the end is best), and include connectives.

Assignment tip

When you write arguments in your assignment, remember that you are not necessarily putting forward your own opinion. You are merely presenting one point of view, as persuasively as you can.

There are different kinds of connective which do different jobs.
- Explaining/giving reasons:
  – *therefore*
  – *because*
  – *so*
  – *the reason for this is …*
  – *it follows that …*

- Supporting/adding to your points:
  – *in addition*
  – *as well*
  – *also*
  – *furthermore*
  – *again, …*
  – *for example*

Structuring your argument

An argument is a well-ordered piece of writing. Your aim is to be as clear and logical as possible, so structure is important. Key aspects of structure in argument texts are as follows.

- The main points are covered in a logical and sensible order.
- Paragraphs are used – a new paragraph for each new point.
- Topic sentences introduce the main point, usually at the beginning of each paragraph; the other sentences develop that point.
- Connectives show the links between the points.
- A powerful beginning and ending are used to make a big impact on the audience.

Activity 18

1 Read the newspaper article on page 33. You are going to explore how good writers structure their arguments. Write answers to the questions about structure in the boxes around the text.

2 Now copy and complete the text skeleton below. Notice how it lists the main points on the left (one per paragraph), and any supporting points or examples on the right.

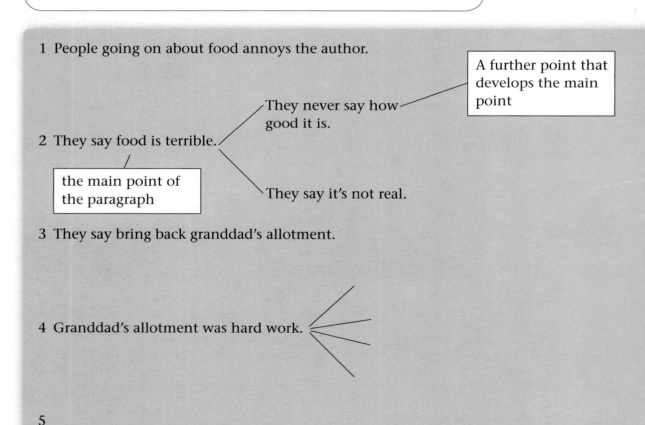

1 People going on about food annoys the author.

A further point that develops the main point

They never say how good it is.

2 They say food is terrible.

the main point of the paragraph

They say it's not real.

3 They say bring back granddad's allotment.

4 Granddad's allotment was hard work.

5

'THE GOOD OLD DAYS'
Were they? Really?

What makes this an effective opening?

Newspaper articles often use very short paragraphs like this. Why? Where else do they occur in this article?

This paragraph is all about Granddad's allotment. Identify the topic sentence that introduces this main point. List three or four other points made to develop the main point in this paragraph.

1 I'll tell you what really annoys me. What really winds me up. It's people going on and on and on about food.

2 They never say how good it is nowadays – that you can buy an uncooked fresh chicken in Tesco's for less than a half-price DVD in a Virgin Megastore – but how terrible it is. Food, apparently, isn't real any more.

3 Bring back granddad's old allotment garden, they say. Bring back the free-range chicken, strutting around after scraps in your own back yard, waking you up at four in the morning.

4 Well, let me tell you about Granddad's allotment, the little slice of land that he and people like him, whose own gardens weren't big enough to swing a cat in, rented from the council so they could grow a few vegetables. It was two miles from where he lived and he'd traipse off there in all weathers to fetch turnips and spuds and cabbages, just to put the veg on my grandmother's table. He hauled a home-made wooden wheel barrow behind his bike. The gastronomic highlight of the week was when grandma opened a tin of salmon if there were visitors on a Sunday for tea. Oh yes, he kept chickens all right. He was close to nature all right. He was truly 'hands on'. He'd force himself to wring their necks when he wanted one for the pot. That's what it means to be 'hands on' and 'close to nature'. That's what they mean when they talk about the 'good old days'.

5 Now I can understand where vegetarians are coming from, and why they go on and on about food. They've got a point. I don't agree with their point, but I have to admit the veggies have got one. What gets me is the middle-class organic meat-eating brigade, those smug people who sneer at the rest of us pushing a trolley round supermarkets and get at us because we're enjoying, yes enjoying, good cheap food. The green-wellie brigade. Those who can afford to buy free-range eggs, chickens that have never been harassed, beef that's been organically fed, never minding the fact it costs three times more than the price that people like me can afford. They bathe the past in a golden glow. When a chance comes along for people not to have to worry about food any more and whether they can afford it, somebody has to bring some worries in. So we have a nation of faddy fussy eaters.

6 Just look at the magazines. They are obsessed with fat. That's what's so unhealthy.

7 And immoral, too. While the rest of the world starves, we in the developed nations are not only eating more than our fair share, we're making a fuss about it. A chicken in Afghanistan costs 110 afghanis, a day's wage. What would people in Afghanistan make of our faddiness? What would granddad say if he could come back? If I told him – 'No more trips to the allotment in the pouring rain, granddad,' do you think he'd mind about that?

8 He'd be as delighted as he was when the council finally plumbed him in and he had his first hot bath. I remember him after it, wrapped in a towel warmed on a radiator, his face aglow with pleasure.

9 'What was all that about the good old days?' he said.

Why has the author used each of the connectives 'but', 'so' and 'too'? Give explanations.

Why do you think the author has written paragraphs of such different lengths?

Is this an effective ending? Explain your answer.

Jack Dawbney, Flipside column,
The Farnham Herald

Activity 19

You are going to write a magazine article with the title 'Fast or posh?' Your article will put forward one side of the argument: is it better to go to a fast food restaurant and eat quickly and cheaply, or pay more to go and eat in a more leisurely (and possibly more healthy) way?

1 Begin by making a plan. Draw a text skeleton like the one you completed on page 32; include three or four main points. You could begin like this:

1 Posh food is better than fast food.

2 Posh restaurants are better than fast food joints. — quieter
— more relaxing

3

4

2 Check that the order of your points is effective. Rearrange the order of your paragraphs if you need to.

3 Now think of a clear and punchy topic sentence for each paragraph. Jot them down on the right of your plan. For example, you could write down this topic sentence for paragraph 1: 'Posh food beats fast food hands down.' You will be completing this activity later.

Assignment tip

Always make a plan before you write. A plan will give your writing structure and purpose. The text skeleton used on page 36 is a good planning tool for writing to argue, persuade or advise.

Practise IT

Cut and Paste
When rearranging the order of your paragraphs you may want to use the cut and paste tool. To do this select one of the paragraphs of text you wish to move and then right-click on it. Select Cut from the pop-up list that appears, the text will disappear. Then place the cursor where you want the text to be placed, right-click again and this time select Paste and the text will reappear.

Using the techniques of argument

Activity 20

A good argument is more than a series of well-structured points. As you read the extract on page 39 (which you'll recognise as being part of the full article on page 37) think about how the writer uses various techniques to put his points across as effectively as possible. Remember these techniques and use them in your own writing.

1 In pairs, discuss the questions around the text; each one refers to a different technique of argument.

2 On your own, find at least one more example of each technique in the rest of the article. Explain what it achieves, and say how effective you think it is. Draw up a chart like the one started below:

Argument technique	Example	What it achieves	How effective
Direct address	'I'll tell you what really annoys me' (para 1).	Grabs the reader at the very start.	Good – it is as if the author is in conversation with you at the start.
Opinion dressed up as fact			

Direct address means using the second person ('you'). What effect does it have here?

Emotive language aims to make the audience feel something strongly. What is the key emotive phrase in this sentence? What does it aim to make you feel?

Just look at the magazines. They are obsessed with fat. That's what's so unhealthy.

And immoral, too. While the rest of the world starves, we in the developed nations are not only eating more than our fair share, we're making a fuss about it. A chicken in Afghanistan costs 110 afghanis, a day's wage. What would people in Afghanistan make of our faddiness? What would granddad say if he could come back? If I told him – 'No more trips to the allotment in the pouring rain, granddad,' do you think he'd mind about that?

The author asks three **rhetorical questions** here. Why?

A **personal anecdote** is a story about the author's own experience. How is it effective here?

These are two **opinions**. Why are they dressed up as facts?

Facts make the author look as if he knows what he is talking about. How does the fact here do this? This sentence is also an **example**. How does this example help the argument?

Activity 21

Return to your plan for 'Fast or posh?' Draft the article, trying to include some of the argument techniques explored above.

Attending to style

Effective communication includes choosing your words well and crafting your sentences. Note the powerful words in the short extract above.

- ***obsessed with fat*** is more powerful than 'They are full of articles about fat.'
- ***faddiness*** is an unusual word, but just right in the context. It contrasts with the harsh reality of life in Afghanistan.
- ***pouring rain*** – the simple addition of 'pouring' adds detail to the picture and weight to the argument.

Activity 22

Crafting sentences means using sentences of different types and different lengths. It also means paying attention to the sound of what you write. Write notes in answer to the following questions, which explore how the writer of the extract above crafts his sentences. You will have the chance to try some of these techniques yourself a little later.

1. The first paragraph consists of three short sentences. What is the effect?

2. Rewrite the sentence below so that it has the same powerful effect.

   The simple fact is that while the rest of the world starves we have got too much food, and we bother ourselves with trivial things – too much fat, salt, sugar and starch, and the wrong kind of fish in our fingers.

3. Identify: (a) a question, (b) a command, and (c) a special sentence (one that isn't grammatically correct). Why has the author used these different types of sentence?

4. The longest sentence is next to the shortest sentence. Is this chance? Explain your answer.

5. The longest sentence is a complex sentence. It shows how ideas are related to each other:

   'While' is the connective that links what people are doing in the developing and developed world.

   While the rest of the world starves, <u>we in the developed nations are not only eating more than our fair share</u>, we're making a fuss about it.

   Note how the commas mark where the three clauses are.

   Rewrite the two sentences below as one sentence, so that the two ideas are linked. Remember to use punctuation to mark the boundaries of the clauses.

   School dinners aren't up to the standard of Jamie Oliver.
   At least they put food on the table.

Activity 23

1 Discuss the draft of your article 'Fast or posh?' with a partner. Suggest ways in which your partner could improve his/her style, by:
   • choosing different words
   • crafting the sentences differently.

2 Redraft your article accordingly.

Thinking about formality and tone

How formal your argument text will be, and what tone you adopt, depends on the precise purpose and audience of the writing.

Activity 24

1 Read the following extract about GM (genetically modified) food from the Prince of Wales' website. The annotations on the left show how he has used very formal language. Those on the right show how he has used a reasonable, unemotional tone.

2 How does the author's choice of formality and tone suit the audience and purpose of the writing?

3 The Prince wants to make the same point to an audience of teenagers. Rewrite the passage for him. Think about how the formality and tone would change. You could begin like this:

I've followed the GM debate very closely for a long time now. And there are still a lot of questions that need to be asked …

'Having followed …' begins the passage in a very formal way.

'I believe' makes the Prince sound very reasonable – it's his opinion, not fact.

'we don't appear to' and 'seem to be' soften the tone and make it reasonable.

Technical and specialised terms used.

Having followed the GM debate very closely for some while now, I believe that there are still a number of unanswered questions which need to be asked.

1 Do we need GM food in this country?
On the basis of what we have seen so far, we don't appear to need it at all. The benefits, such as there are, seem to be limited to the people who own the technology and the people who farm on an industrialised scale. We are constantly told that this technology may have huge benefits for the future. Well, perhaps. But we have all heard claims like that before and they don't always come true in the long run – look at the case of antibiotic growth promoters in animal foodstuff …

Most of the sentences are complex and lengthy.

'perhaps' allows for the possibility that the opposition are right.

source: www.princeofwales.gov.uk

Countering the opposition

One special technique that writers of argument texts use is to refer to the argument of the opposition at times. This is called a counter-argument. You can use a counter-argument in different ways:
- to contradict it, or prove it wrong, giving reasons
- to exaggerate or distort it, to show how wrong it is
- to allow a small point from the other side, which makes you seem reasonable.

Note that some connectives are very useful when signalling to the audience that you are contradicting an argument:
- *however*
- *but*
- *yet*
- *on the other hand*
- *yes … but …*
- *although*

Activity 25

The text below comes from a magazine article entitled 'How dare you say junk'. Look closely at the counter-arguments, which are highlighted in yellow in this article and in the Prince of Wales' argument on page 37. Then answer the questions below.

1 Where are counter-arguments simply stated? How does the writer argue against each one?

2 Where does the writer allow a small point to the opposition? What connective signposts this?

Junk food, they say. There is no such thing as junk food. It's a contradiction. Food is what keeps us alive. How can it be written off in this way?
Yes, some foods may be better for our health than others. But we can all make ourselves ill by eating too much of any one thing, just as Morgan Spurlock did in his film *Supersize Me* to make his point against a fast food chain. He ate nothing but burgers for months. He would have sickened just the same if he'd eaten nothing but watercress.

Key points

An effective argument consists of:
- a clearly stated conclusion
- a series of points that are connected and developed
- a well-planned structure, using paragraphs, topic sentences and connectives
- techniques such as emotive language, direct address, facts and opinions, rhetorical questions and counter-arguments
- attention to style, especially choice of vocabulary and varied sentence structure
- a formality and tone that suit the audience and purpose of the writing.

Activity 26

Practise all that you have learnt in this section by writing the argument text described below.

You have returned with your school from a residential weekend at a youth hostel. Although the hostel itself was quite comfortable and clean, you and your fellow pupils were very unhappy with the food – both the amount and the quality. Mild complaints made through the teachers got you nowhere. You decide to write a letter of complaint to the manager of the hostel, arguing your case. Follow these steps.

1 Think about the points you want to make. You will have to invent some details: what was wrong with the food, exactly? Here are some possibilities.
   - The food had gone cold.
   - There was not enough of it.
   - It was badly served up.

2 Plan your argument. Draw up a skeleton (see page 32) listing the main points on the left and any supporting points on the right (you can add to these later). Think about the order of your points. Can you start and end with a powerful point? Add some effective topic sentences to your plan.

3 Add some facts, opinions, emotive language, direct address and rhetorical questions. Make sure your facts sound accurate – e.g. if the chips were cold, when? Can you use any quotations?

4 Think about what could be said by 'the other side' and come up with some counter-arguments. It might be said, for example, that you did not visit the hostel to eat gourmet meals, that you have not paid enough, that you have no right to stand up and complain like this. How will you answer points like these?

5 Get your formality and tone right. Think about the purpose and audience of your writing. You don't want to sound loud-mouthed and aggressive, but at the same time you want to come across as purposeful and having something to say. Consider whether humour is appropriate. Think about the best way of speaking not just for yourself, but on behalf of everybody staying at the hostel.

6 Write your letter; remember to set it out as a formal letter.

7 When you check your letter, look especially at:
   - the choice of words – can you improve any of them?
   - your sentence structure – can you add variety and impact?
   - spelling, punctuation and grammar.

Practise IT

Alignment
When writing your letter you will need to place the address of the person who is receiving it in the top-right hand corner (see page 120). To do this you can press the TAB key (usually above Caps Lock) until the cursor is on the right hand side of the screen. Remember to leave enough space to type in the address though! You will need to do this for each line.

2 Writing to persuade

My learning

In 'Writing to persuade' I will:
- *learn about the key features of writing to persuade*
- *write persuasive texts, thinking about language, content and structure*
- *explore the rhetorical techniques that persuasive texts use*
- *take account of audience and purpose in my writing.*

When you write to persuade, your aim is to persuade the audience to do something or believe something. Typical examples are adverts, political speeches and newspaper editorials. Many of their features are similar to those of argument texts. However, there is usually a stronger appeal to the reader's feelings and more emphasis on the power of language.

Writing to fit the audience and purpose

Assignment tip

In the assignment you will be asked to write a piece that combines more than one purpose, for example argue, persuade and advise. Writing to persuade uses many of the same features and techniques as writing to argue and writing to advise.

Activity 27

Read Advert A below and Advert B on page 41. The table at the top of page 41 analyses some of the key features of Advert A; draw up a similar table for Advert B.

Fad Free
Weight Loss

Don't Diet this year - learn how to eat healthily and take control.

If you've been on the diet see-saw for more years than you care to remember - now's the time to jump off and take control once and for all.

You don't have to follow strict plans or risky regimes, or force down special diet foods. The simple truth is that small changes in your eating, drinking and lifestyle habits will help you lose weight steadily and keep it off.

Here's three resources with the information and tools to help you learn how to eat well and stay slim for life.

New for 2006

Nutrition Info for 21,000 Foods
Essential for the slimmer's bookshelf, this brand new edition of the Calorie Bible gives calories, protein, carbs, fat and fibre in over 21,000 foods - including a new eating out section. Values are given for popular serving sizes and per 100g making it easy to compare different foods.

How Many Calories You Need
Tables and charts show you how many calories you need, how many extra you burn during exercise, your body mass index and healthy weight range.

How to Lose Weight
Top dietitian, Juliette Kellow spills the beans on fad diets, and gives you the know-how and strategies needed to lose weight and keep it off.

"What a brilliant book, I know I'll be sinking my teeth into it regularly!"
Amanda Ursell

the **calorie carb fatbible 2006**
The UK's Most Comprehensive Calorie Counter

The Calorie, Carb & Fat Bible is £12.99. Available from bookshops, by phone on 01733 345592, or online at www.dietandfitnessresources.co.uk

	Advert A
1 Who is it aimed at?	Women aged 20–40
2 How do you know?	Photo Description of dieting for years
3 What is the purpose of the ad?	To persuade readers to buy the *Calorie, Carb & Fat Bible*.
4 What does it make you want to feel?	That you can lose weight and improve your lifestyle safely
5 How does the language do this?	It highlights the potential ease – 'small changes', 'don't have to follow strict plans' It's very positive – 'stay slim for life' It's friendly/informal – 'jump off', 'simple truth' The tone is light/fun – 'diet see-saw', 'spills the beans'

Advert B, from *Top Santé* Magazine

© Salus

Note that the writer of Advert B uses more formal language. It suits the purpose of the advert, and it suits the audience the writer is aiming to persuade.

Activity 28

Imagine that you run a curry house. You are trying to attract customers away from the fish and chip café next door, so you are writing an advert to put in your window.

1 In pairs brainstorm some selling points – for example, your food tastes better, is more healthy, is more interesting …

2 One of you should write an ad aimed at young people; make this light in tone and informal. The other should write an ad aimed at older people; make this more serious and formal. In each case, think about what you want the audience to feel.

3 Swap your adverts and discuss (a) how they are similar, and (b) how they are different.

Speaking and listening

Speaking and listening opportunity

AO1(ii) *Participate in discussion by both speaking and listening. Judge the nature and purposes of contributions and the roles of participants*
This is a **discussion-based** activity. It will be used to assess how well you can **discuss/argue/persuade**.

1 'Adverts get us to buy things we don't want by making us feel we cannot do without a product. This is emotional blackmail.'
Discuss this statement, referring to the adverts on these pages as well as others that are currently in the media.
2 Record the results of your discussion. Appoint a spokesperson to feed back the results to the class.

To gain good marks you need to:
- *play a leading part in the discussion*
- *make good contributions that are well-expressed*
- *listen sensitively, and show that you can work well as part of a group*
- *challenge constructively, building on points made by others.*

Using rhetorical techniques

Rhetorical techniques are methods used by writers to persuade their audience.

Activity 29

Read the political speech below, which comes from George Orwell's famous novel *Animal Farm*. At first sight it looks like a children's book with talking animals (the speaker here is a pig). However, it has a much more serious purpose – the speaker is stirring up his audience for a revolution.

The rhetorical techniques used by the speaker are listed below. Match them up with the letters in the margins.

1　Rhetorical question to engage the audience.
2　Use of 'we' and 'our' (first person) to include the audience.
3　A sudden short sentence to make the audience take notice.
4　Use of 'you' (second person), called direct address.
5　Emotive language – words used to make the audience feel something strongly.
6　Exaggeration, to make his points even more persuasive.
7　Powerful statement to begin speech.
8　A list of three – a powerful way of giving examples.
9　Repetition of sentence structure to pile up examples.

A

C

B

D

E

F

G

Man is the only creature that consumes without producing. He does not give milk, he does not lay eggs, he is too weak to pull the plough, he cannot run fast enough to catch rabbits. Yet he is lord of all the animals. He sets them to work, he gives back to them the bare minimum that will prevent them from starving, and the rest he keeps for himself. Our labour tills the soil, our dung fertilizes it, and yet there is not one of us that owns more than his bare skin. You cows that I see before me, how many thousands of gallons of milk have you given during this last year? And what has happened to that milk which should have been breeding up sturdy calves? Every drop of it has gone down the throats of our enemies.

H

I

Note how the audience is addressed directly with a series of rhetorical questions. The speaker is not expecting them to tell him, literally, how many gallons of milk there were. It's a more effective way of saying: 'You have given thousands of gallons of milk during this last year.'

Other ways of asking rhetorical questions are:

- 'Surely …?'
- 'Aren't you …?'
- 'What could be more …?'

Activity 30

1 You are going to write a leaflet advertising barbecues for sale. You want to begin with a rhetorical question to draw the reader in – jot down three or four. You may like to use these sentence starters:

'Surely one of the joys of …'
'What could be more pleasant than …'
'Don't you want …?'

2 Share your sentences in small groups and discuss which one is the most effective.

Thinking about sound

Speeches are meant to be heard rather than read. A good speech will take into account the sound of the words and sentences. You have already noted some ways in which the speech in *Animal Farm* does this:
- by repeating the same word or phrase
- by using a list of three, which gives a sentence an effective rhythm.

Other sound effects that persuasive writers use are:
- alliteration, such as 'Fad Free' and 'risky regimes' (in the Weight loss advert)
- rhyming/assonance, e.g.: 'It's not a mad law, just a bad law.'

Activity 31

You are about to address a rally of people protesting against factory farming. You have written down notes for your final sentence or two:

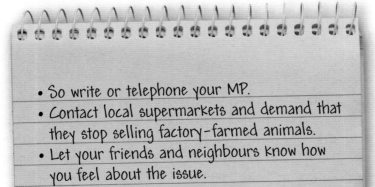

- So write or telephone your MP.
- Contact local supermarkets and demand that they stop selling factory-farmed animals.
- Let your friends and neighbours know how you feel about the issue.

Turn these notes into a powerful ending for your speech which rouses the audience to action. You may have to alter a lot of the words and structure the sentences differently. Use at least two of the sound effects explored above.

Using emotive words and ideas

You can make your writing more persuasive by including emotive words and ideas, or images.

Activity 32

Read the following extract, which is taken from an editorial in a popular newspaper. It is objecting to GM (genetically modified) foods. (Frankenstein was the scientist in Mary Shelley's novel of the same name who created a monster.)

1 Describe the image of scientists that the writer is drawing.

2 What does the writer want to make you feel about scientists?

3 Which words in this extract are the most emotive? Give your reasons.

Frankenstein food

Genetically modified tomatoes and oranges are about to be let loose on an unsuspecting public. What on earth are the scientists doing to our food?

Those men in white coats, in hissing laboratories, are unleashing unnatural and destructive powers. They are distorting nature.

Whatever is wrong with the good old-fashioned tomato, as God meant it to be?

But 'good' and 'God' don't seem to be words in the scientists' vocabulary. Or 'right' and 'wrong'. It's all about progress. And unheard-of profits.

Activity 33

A different newspaper wants to praise scientists for the research they are doing into GM crops. It believes that GM crops will solve the world's food problems. Write the first few sentences of this piece.

Choose one of the following ideas, or images, of scientists.
• Fearless and energetic life-savers.
• Detectives who work to solve the 'crime' of world hunger.

Think of some emotive words and phrases to go with these images and draft your opening. Give your piece a punchy title.

Activity 34

Practise all that you have learnt in this section by trying this piece of persuasive writing.

You are working for a new charity, called Start the Day, which organises teams of volunteers to provide free breakfasts for homeless people in London. You are writing the 'What you can do' page of the charity's website.

1 Think of two or three things that you want your audience to do, such as donating money to pay for the rent of local halls, or volunteering to cook and serve food.

2 Then plan two or three paragraphs of writing. Use the planning diagram that you used when writing to argue (see page 34).

3 Draft your piece, thinking always about your audience. What kind of people are they? How can you speak directly to them? Adapt your tone and formality to suit this audience.

4 Include some rhetorical techniques, especially emotive words and images.

5 Make sure you begin and end your page with maximum impact. If you can use the same phrase or idea in both the beginning and end, it ties the piece together neatly.

6 Read through your writing when you have finished. Would it persuade you? Check grammar, spelling and punctuation.

Assignment tip

If you have been asked to write a leaflet or web page, don't be tempted to spend time on the design. Focus on the writing, and, if necessary, on use of headings, bold and bullet points.

Key points

Key features of writing to persuade are:
- close attention to audience and purpose, especially when getting the tone and formality right
- using rhetorical techniques such as repetition, direct address, rhetorical questions
- beginning and ending in a way that will grab the audience's attention
- sound effects, especially if you are writing a speech
- using emotive words and images.

Writing to advise

My learning

In 'Writing to advise' I will:
- learn about the key features of writing to advise
- look at the language used in advice texts
- explore how important structure is in advice texts
- take account of audience and purpose in my writing.

When you write to advise, you are trying to get the audience to act in a particular way. This is not for your own benefit (as in writing to persuade), but for theirs. Advice is given on everything from bicycle maintenance to getting on with your girlfriend/boyfriend. Advice texts can be found in books, on the Internet, in leaflets and on the problem pages of magazines.

Looking at language

Activity 35

Read Text 1 below and Text 2 on page 48, which are Magazine articles containing advice. Identify the language features of advice texts by copying and completing the table on page 48.

Text 1

Worried Meat Eater

Q My daughter has just started at secondary school and has come home with the idea that she wants to be a veggie. Neither my husband nor myself or the rest of my family can understand it as we all enjoy a Sunday roast and have always thought that our daughter enjoyed eating with us and doing things together as a family. Now it seems she wants to be different. What should I do?

Anxious parent

A Don't panic! Your daughter is not refusing to be part of your family. She is showing you she is an individual with a mind of her own. You say in your letter that she has 'come home with the idea' that she wants to be a vegetarian. From the way you say this I don't think you are taking her seriously – you believe this is a passing fad, a rather silly idea she has picked up somewhere. Why don't you talk to her and see what ideas are in her mind? Take them seriously. Go along with her and try cooking a vegetarian dish for the family. Even better, you could get her to cook one for you. If you simply block her wishes, your relationship will suffer.

I'm not suggesting that your whole family turn vegetarian overnight. I don't suppose you ever will. But it worries me that you seem to dismiss your daughter's ideas so readily. Do you put her down on other matters too? And one word of caution: drop the dismissive term 'veggie'.

Feature of advice text	Text A	Text B
Direct address (use of second person)	Your daughter …	
Conversational, informal tone		Relax a bit …
Clear points of advice		
Reasons why advice should be followed	She is showing you …	
Causal connective signposting the reason		If you're truly worried …
Understands the feelings/ position of the audience		
Offers comfort/reassurance		
Opinions given		
A challenge or warning to the reader		

Assignment tip

When writing to advise, don't worry about including features from other text types. Advice often contains instructions, information, reasons and persuasive techniques. You may be asked in the assignment to combine several different purposes in one piece of writing.

Text 2

Annabel Goldstaub says …

If you would dearly love to be thin but aren't, ask yourself why. It's easy to believe that if you were slimmer your life would change instantly. But waiting to be thin in order to find the perfect job, pass your exams, take care of your appearance or find yourself a boyfriend is just a waste of time.

Relax a bit … Take a permanent break from strict dieting. It never served in making you happy anyway, did it? If you're truly worried about your shape and eating habits, talk it out with a sympathetic friend or go and see your doctor.

Learn to be happy with yourself the way you are and don't let society pressurise you into being a shape that isn't right for *you*.

Commands and suggestions

When writing advice, you may want to give straightforward intsructions to the reader. In other words, *commands*:
• 'Don't panic', 'Learn to be happy with yourself'.

To soften the effect of too many commands, you could include other methods as well:
• **modal verbs** (*could, would, might, ought,* etc), e.g. 'You could get her to cook one for you'
• **conditionals** ('*if … then*'), e.g. 'If you're truly worried about your shape and eating habits, talk it out …'
• **questions/suggestions**, e.g. 'Why don't you talk to her and see what ideas are in her mind?'

Activity 36

Soften the following commands by rewriting each of them in at least two different ways.

1 Add grated carrots or chopped celery to mince when making burgers.

2 Drink at least eight glasses of water a day.

3 Ditch the chocolate bar and make a banana your mid-morning snack.

Activity 37

You are an advice column writer for a magazine. Reply to the letter below, using some of the techniques you have been exploring.

I am so worried about my friend. He used to have a good appetite, and a normal attitude to food. But now he never seems to eat anything, and fusses about calories and everything. He is getting thinner and thinner and is obsessed with exercising. He looks really ill. What can I do?

Seb

Lightening the message

The advice texts explored so far have been quite serious and formal in tone. Whether you use a serious or a lighter tone will depend on the purpose and audience of the advice.

Activity 38

Read the advice on page 50, which comes from from *Health Plus* magazine. Discuss the following with a partner.

1 Where has the writer included a lighter, less formal tone?

2 Why has the writer done this? How effective is it?

3 Imagine you are the writer of the article, and you want to include a paragraph on the benefits of olive oil. So far, you have some rather dry, factual notes on a Post-it. Turn these into a paragraph that will fit with the tone of 'Eat to beat pain'. You could begin, 'Hot-off-the-press research from the University of Pennsylvania …'

Eat to Beat Pain

We all know a balanced diet plays a big part in keeping us healthy and helping to ward off illness, but did you know that food can also help you beat pain?

Some foods actually contain potent pain-relieving properties, which are gaining increasing support from science. Although you're not likely to find your pharmacist throwing out the aspirin to make room for oily fish and chilli peppers, the fact remains that some foods can help treat a whole host of pain conditions, from arthritis to headaches and even back pain. All you need to do is treat your food as medicine on a plate.

Olive oil

- New scientific research suggests extra-virgin olive oil can help to fight inflammation.
- Experts at University of Pennsylvania have discovered that good-quality olive oil contains a compound, oleocanthal, which suppresses pain. It uses same pathway as anti-inflammatory agents such as ibuprofen.
- May explain why Mediterranean diet is so healthy – studies show decreased risk of heart disease and stroke.
- Regular use of olive oil could be good for you.

Looking at structure

When writing to advise, you must pay close attention to structure and layout. You are trying to get someone to do something, so you need to guide them through the steps in a logical but attractive way.

Activity 39

Read 'Fed up with school dinners?' (page 51), which is taken from a government website aimed at teenagers. Write notes on the following questions about structure and layout. Remember these techniques so that you can use them in the writing task that follows on page 52.

1 In what **order** has the writer decided to put her tips? Why?

2 How has she grabbed the reader's attention at the **start**?

3 Is the **end** effective? Give your reasons.

4 The **paragraphs** are usually one or two sentences long. Why?

5 Many of the paragraphs begin with **topic sentences**. What do these do?

6 How do the **subheadings** help to make the text easier to read? Comment also on the wording of the headings.

7 What is the purpose of the **images**?

Fed up with school dinners?

And think packed lunches are boring too? Well think again! Why not spend a few minutes putting some packed lunch ideas together?

And remember to add what you need to the weekly shopping list.

Packing your lunch can be done in five minutes in the morning before school.

Or, if you're usually pushed for time in the morning, pack it the night before and put it in the fridge. But don't forget to take it with you in the morning!

And if you struggle to eat breakfast before school – then why not pack some breakfast as well?

Getting started

Start your packed lunch off with some starchy carbohydrate to give you long-lasting energy. For a change from ordinarybread you could try:

- pittas
- bagels
- baguettes
- ciabatta
- crackers
- rolls
- rice cakes

Make some of them wholemeal or multigrain, or use a mixture of wholegrain and white.

And then

Add some protein, such as lean meat, fish or cheese, and a few vegetables and fruit.

Here are a few filling ideas to try, or you could make up your own combinations:

- cheddar cheese with apple slices
- tuna, cucumber, green pepper, sweetcorn and tomato
- cooked chicken or turkey, mustard, tomatoes, and lettuce
- mozzarella with grilled peppers
- cottage cheese and dried apricots
- brie and cranberry sauce or jam

You could also raid the fridge for leftovers – some foods taste just as good cold – such as pizza or pasta. Cook extra pasta, couscous or rice. Mix it with cut-up vegetables, a few nuts or tuna, then just add your favourite dressing.

Take a tempting dip, such as houmous, cottage cheese or plain yoghurt with some red or green pesto stirred in for extra interest; or you could chop an apple into a mashed can of tuna. Have some sticks of celery, carrots or pepper, or some cauliflower and broccoli with the dips.

Add some fruit to help fill you up (and help you reach your 5-a-day). Try to have a different type every day – you don't always need to pick an orange and an apple; why not try kiwi, mango, grapes, pear, chunks of melon, or small packets of dried fruit?

Include treats from time to time (but ideally not every day), such as a flapjack, a slice of cake, or the occasional fun-size chocolate bar. The same goes for crisps, which are high in fat and salt; and fizzy drinks, which are high in sugar.

And to drink

The best drink is water or milk, but you could try flavoured spring waters, diluted fruit juices or flavoured milks if you prefer, or to make a change.

And don't forget to keep your packed lunch cool. Use a frozen carton of juice or icepacks to keep it cool, or find somewhere cool at school to keep your lunchbox.

For more ideas for a healthy lunchbox click here to check out these lunchbox ideas. This bit is written for parents, but you might find some of it useful.

Activity 40

Use all the techniques you have explored and practised so far in this section to plan and write a short advice leaflet called 'Boost your energy'. Its purpose is to give teenagers tips on how eating the right foods can give them the energy they need for daily life. Follow these steps.

1 Discuss with a partner what effect the audience and purpose of this leaflet will have on your style. Think about tone, formality and use of humour.

2 Brainstorm three or four main points that you want to make. If you run out of ideas, you could borrow some of these:
   • don't skip breakfast
   • eat regular meals
   • eat food with iron content
   • keep drinking water.

3 Then plan three or four paragraphs of writing. Use the planning diagram that you used when writing to argue (see page 34).

4 Draft your leaflet, thinking always about your audience. Adapt your tone and formality to suit this audience.

5 Include some key language features of advice texts, e.g. reasons for your advice, understanding of the audience, direct address and modal verbs.

6 Make sure the structure and layout are clear and attractive.

7 Read through your writing when you have finished. Would you take this advice? Check grammar, spelling and punctuation.

Key points

Key features of writing to advise are:
• close attention to audience and purpose, especially when getting the tone and formality right
• language features such as direct address, conversational tone and offering reassurance
• clear points of advice that are developed, giving reasons
• close attention to the structure and layout of the advice.

Practise IT

Spellchecker
You can check the spelling of your written work using your PC's spellchecker. First select Tools from the top of the screen, then Spelling and Grammar. Any misspelled words will be highlighted and it may suggest some replacements. It is wise not to rely completely on the spellchecker as it will not highlight where your spelling is correct but you have used the wrong word. You will also need to check that the spell checker is set to UK English rather than US English. Always read through your work yourself.

C Assignment practice: Reading media texts and writing to argue, persuade, advise

In your assignment for Unit 1B you will have one complete assignment covering:
- Reading media texts
- Writing to argue, persuade, advise
- Reading non-fiction texts
- Writing to inform, explain, describe

You will already have studied the media and non-fiction texts which will be on the same theme. You will have a total of four hours in which to do the complete assignment. The four tasks in Unit 1B are together worth 30% of your final mark for Single Award GCSE English or English Studies.

The following assignment gives you the opportunity to practise the skills you have been learning for reading media texts and writing to argue, persuade, advise. There is also detailed guidance on how to tackle this practice assignment on pages 58–60.

On pages 109–114 you will find the practice assignment for the second part:
- Reading non-fiction texts
- Writing to inform, explain, describe

In your **Reading** responses you need to show that you:
- understand the texts and their meaning
- can describe how language, structure and presentational devices are used for specific effects
- can back up your analysis by making detailed reference to the texts
- can make effective comparisons between texts.

In your **Writing** responses you need to show that:
- you can communicate your ideas clearly and imaginatively
- you can write for a particular purpose and audience
- you can organise your ideas in sentences and paragraphs
- you can use words and sentence structures effectively
- your spelling and punctuation are accurate.

HEALTHY EATING FOR SCHOOLS

You have a maximum of 4 hours to complete all the tasks below and on page 110.

You must study the following media texts in order to complete this task.

1 Three pages from the celebrity chef Jamie Oliver's Feed Me Better website:
- home page
- Why Feed Me Better?
- Manifesto for Change

2 One page fro the World Health Organisation website.

3 Two pages from the website My School Lunch:
- home page
- 'Why should I choose a school lunch for my child?'

Stage 1: Analysing the texts
You are a member of the school council. You have been asked to investigate designing a website for the school council, which would cover concerns of students, such as school dinners. You have been given some media texts to look at.

Task 1
Write a review of the websites, identifying the techniques that they use to advise their aims. Your review will help your school council make its own website effective. You must study the websites listed above in order to write your review. For your review you must select **only two** of these websites. In your review you should compare the material from your two websites by:
- identifying the techniques that are being used to encourage healthy eating
- commenting on the visual/design techniques
- commenting on the language used in your chosen websites.

You must refer closely to the **two** websites throughout and must include example from these websites in order to illustrate the points that you are making.
In this task you will be assessed for your reading skills.

(20 marks for Reading)

Task 2
Your school has now adopted a healthy eating policy, which it is promoting on the new school council website. Write a letter from the school council to parents persuading them
- to let their children have school dinners
- that the healthy eating policy should be put into practice at home.

Support your points with material from **ANY** of the websites provided and anything else you know about healthy eating.

You will be assessed for your skills in writing to **argue**, **persuade** and **advise**.

(20 marks for Writing)

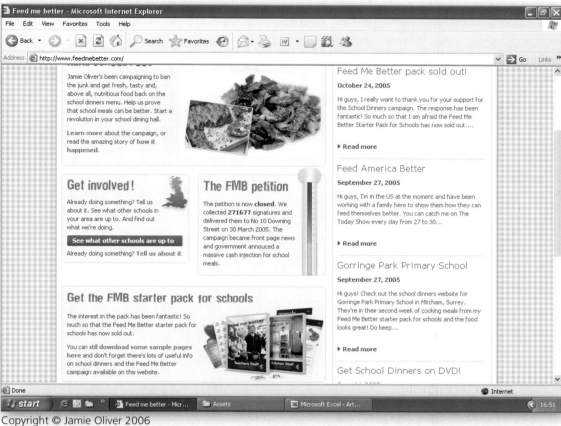

Copyright © Jamie Oliver 2006

Copyright © Jamie Oliver 2006

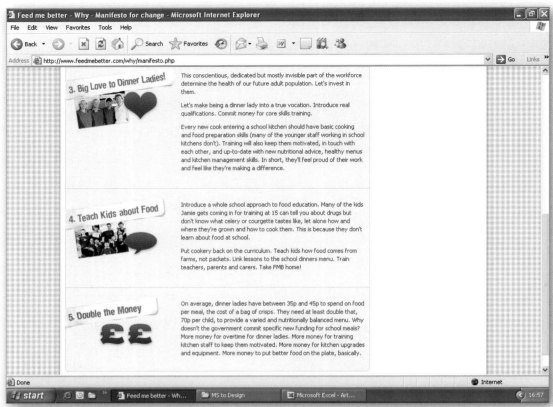

Copyright © Jamie Oliver 2006

Directgov
www.direct.gov.uk

Cymraeg | Accessibility | Help | Site index | Contacts

Search this site [   ] [Go ➡]

Young people

Healthy Eating
No matter how much exercise you do, eating fatty junk foods seven days a week can damage your body.

Keeping healthy

What's healthy?
Healthy eating is all about making sure you get the recommended amounts of vitamins, minerals, protein and carbohydrates, as well as the right types of fats and sugars.

There's a huge amount of healthy eating advice and information about, and trying to get your head around all of it is almost impossible. But if you do think your diet could be improved, there are a few simple things to remember.

A healthy diet
Making sure that you're eating the right balance of the right foods is the key to a healthy diet. Here are a few top tips to make sure that you're having the right mix of foods:
- eat at least five portions of fruit and vegetables every day. This includes servings of fruit juice and baked beans
- base your meals on starchy foods, such as potatoes, brown rice and wholemeal bread
- if you eat meat every day of the week, try substituting it with oily fish like mackerel, salmon or tuna on a couple of days
- always go for low-fat cheese, milk and yoghurt
- watch how much salt you're eating. As most salt we eat comes from processed foods, read the label – food containing more than 1.25 grams of salt per 100g is a lot. Don't add it to food when you're cooking or at the table
- try and cut down the number high fat or high sugar snacks and drinks you have every week

Do in online
▶ Find health services in your area
▶ Claim health treatment in Europe (European Health Insurance Card, formerly E111)
▶ Get help covering health costs (leaflet HC11)

Useful contacts
▶ NHS Direct
▶ Talk to FRANK
▶ ASH
▶ Eating Disorder Association
▶ Young people contacts

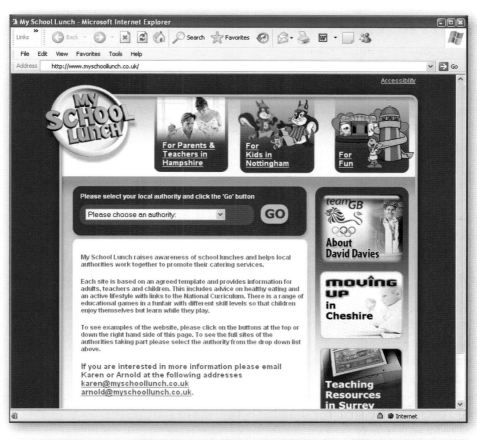

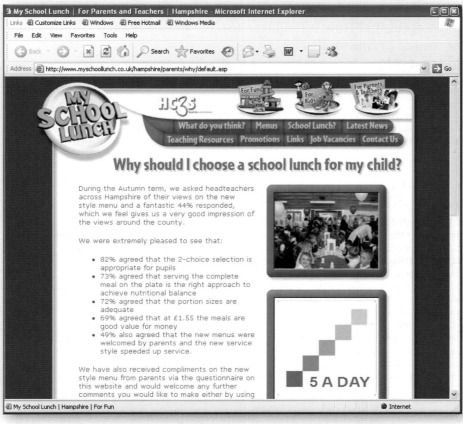

Assignment advice

Before you start

You have been given three media texts. In the actual assignment you will have studied these in class before seeing the assessment tasks. Here you haven't had that luxury! Instead, this gives you the opportunity to practise some basic reading
skills – skimming and summarising.

In your actual GCSE assessment you can make notes during the assessment. You are not allowed, however, to take these notes out of the assessment room. You are not allowed to take notes or annotated versions of the texts into the assessment room.

Scan each of the three texts in turn. Draw up a table on a large sheet of paper to record some basic details on each one.
Include the following.
- **Purpose and audience**. What is the main aim of each text, and who is it addressing?
- **Structure**. How are the texts structured? Include (a) how they link to other texts, (b) the structural features that form part of the text, and (c) how the words are put together on the page.
- **Language**. What are the distinctive features of the language? Is it full of facts or opinions? How is language used to persuade or inform? How formal or informal is it?
- **Presentational devices**. How are the words, illustrations and overall design presented? How effective are the presentational devices.

Stage 1: Analysing the texts

Task 1
You have been asked to write a review comparing two of the websites. Your first job is to choose which two texts. Look back over your notes and choose the texts that you have most to say about.

The task has been broken up into three parts:
- identify the techniques that are being used to encourage healthy eating
- commenting on the visual/design techniques
- commenting on the language used in your chosen websites.

When you identify techniques, such as the use of facts and opinions, you need to back up your comments by referring to the texts.

When you compare the websites, you need to look at their similarities and differences.

In both cases you should include your own comments on how well (or badly) the texts fulfil their purposes.

You need to decide whether you are going to tackle all three parts of the review together or separately.

You could follow either of these two plans.

Plan 1
- Begin with a short introduction, saying what you are going to do and why.
- Identify techniques and evaluate the first text you have chosen.
- Identify techniques and evaluate the second text.
- End with a conclusion that focuses on comparing the two texts.

Plan 2
- Begin with a short introduction, saying what you are going to do and why.
- Briefly summarise techniques in the first text you have chosen.
- Briefly summarise techniques in the second text.
- Compare and evaluate both texts together.
- End with a short conclusion.

Discuss with a partner the advantages and disadvantages of each method. Then decide which plan you are going to follow.

Note that in Stage 1 you are being assessed for your reading skills. You have been 'put in role' as a member of the school council and you have to show that you understand the texts and can say interesting and useful things about them.

You still have to write in continuous prose, however. Notes are not acceptable.

Task 2
Here you are being assessed on the quality of your writing. You have been given a single writing task. Before you start planning, you need to 'get into role'. Think about:
- who you are supposed to be
- why you are writing (purpose)
- who you are writing for (audience)
- how this will affect the content and style of your writing.

In particular, you should think about these questions.
- What arguments have you got in favour of school dinners and for following healthy eating at home?
- How formal will the writing be? How reasonable, or emotional, will the writing be?

The writing is to be done in the form of a letter. Jot down three or four key features of letter writing to remind you to write to this format.

Remember that you are being assessed for your skills in writing for three particular purposes: to **argue**, **persuade**, **advise**.
- You must 'persuade parents to let their children have school dinners'. Here you are trying to **persuade** your audience. Jot down some key features of writing to persuade, to remind you to write to this purpose.
- In the second part of the letter you need to argue a case. Jot down three or four key features of writing to **argue**, to remind you to write to this purpose.

Here is a possible plan for your writing.
1 An introduction outlining who you are and why you are writing.
2 A section persuading parents to support the school dinner policy.
3 A section arguing that the healthy eating policy should be used at home.
4 A conclusion.

Now write your letter. Remember to:
- use paragraphs
- check your writing carefully at the end (is it effective?; have you kept 'in role'?)
- check the spelling, grammar and punctuation
- check that you have written in the format of a letter.

If you are keying in your final draft, check it one more time. Typing mistakes and other errors creep in when you type. Do not rely on a spellchecking device.

Checklist of learning

Reading media texts

1 Understanding structure
- You need to be able to comment on how media texts are structured.
- Structure includes how the texts are put together and the way the words are positioned on the page.
- Texts are structured differently depending on audience and purpose.
- Some media texts are structured to allow the audience to interact with them.

2 Understanding language
- Facts and opinions can both be used to influence the audience.
- Key ingredients of persuasive language include powerful verbs and adjectives, asking questions, repetition and other sound effects, first and second person pronouns, and commands.
- Media texts often use emotive language to help get their message across.
- The formality of language in media texts varies depending on its audience and purpose.

3 Understanding presentation
- Media texts rely on their visual appearance far more than word-based texts.
- Visual images, like words, are chosen very carefully for maximum effect.
- Presentational devices include the way words are presented (headings, style and size of font, use of bold, etc.), the illustrations (photos, graphics) and the overall design, including colour.
- When you compare the presentational devices used in media texts you must be as careful and logical as when you compare their words.

Writing to argue, persuade, advise

1 Writing to argue
An effective argument consists of:
- a clearly stated conclusion
- a series of points that are connected and developed
- a well-planned structure, using paragraphs, topic sentences and connectives
- techniques such as emotive language, direct address, facts and opinions, rhetorical questions and counter-arguments
- attention to style, especially choice of vocabulary and varied sentence structure
- a formality and tone that suits the audience and purpose of the writing.

2 Writing to persuade
Key features of writing to persuade are:
- close attention to the audience and purpose, especially when getting the tone and formality right
- using rhetorical techniques such as repetition, direct address, rhetorical questions
- beginning and ending in a way that will grab the audience's attention
- sound effects, especially if you are writing a speech
- using emotive words and images.

3 Writing to advise
Key features of writing to advise are:
- close attention to the audience and purpose, especially when getting the tone and formality right
- language features such as direct address, conversational tone and offering reassurance
- clear points of advice which are developed, giving reasons
- close attention to the structure and layout of the advice.

Non-fiction

My learning

In this section I will:
- *learn how to approach the non-fiction section of Unit 1B (pages 65–66)*
- *learn and practise the skills in reading non-fiction texts and writing to inform, explain, describe (pages 69–108)*
- *practise speaking and listening activities for Unit 1A*
- *have a go at a sample assignment, with help from the assignment advice (pages 109–117).*

Introduction

What are non-fiction texts?

In the second half of the assignment you will be reading and writing about non-fiction texts. A non-fiction text is any that is not made up; it is not fiction or poetry. The term non-fiction covers all sorts of texts that present facts, opinions, explanations and descriptions.

Activity 1

The table below need examples. The first column lists some types of non-fiction text. The purpose of each of these types is given in the second column, and some examples are listed below the table. The examples are not in the correct order. Reorder the examples and put them in the table so that it makes sense.

Text type	Purpose
Recount	To help the reader understand why or how something is as it is.
Information	To help someone understand an issue by presenting arguments and information from different viewpoints.
Instruction	To present facts in a way that is easy to understand.
Explanation	To sell an idea or a product, to advise on a course of action, or to argue for a particular view.
Persuasion	To tell someone clearly how to do something, through a series of sequenced steps.
Discussion	To tell the reader what happened, often in an informative and entertaining way.

Examples

Thunderstorms usually occur when moist air rises. In summer this is often triggered by the ground becoming very warm …

A new study comparing 1960s lifestyles with today's trends has discovered that women have gained on average an extra 90 minutes in bed on a Sunday morning and no longer get up before men.

One day I remember experiencing weather like I had never seen before. One minute there was brilliant sunshine …

Follow these steps to view the CD-ROM.
• Insert the CD-ROM into your CD-ROM drive.
• Double-click the HCT.pdf icon …

Those in favour of single-sex schools point to the apparently higher league-table performances of such schools. Those who favour co-educational schools, however, point out that …

If you are being bullied you MUST tell someone you can trust:
• your mum, dad or carer
• a friend
• a teacher.

Real texts don't always fall neatly into the categories above. For example, a text aimed at persuading you not to take drugs may contain a lot of information; it may also contain some personal recount.

Non-fiction texts may include autobiography, personal records, viewpoints on society, travel writing, reportage and letters. They can be found in a wide variety of sources, including newspapers, magazines, books, leaflets and the Internet.

The reading skills you will be assessed on

The texts that you will be given for your assignment will all contain arguments. They may be written by a newspaper columnist who wants to put across a point of view in a persuasive way. Or the emphasis may be more on entertaining the reader. In some texts, the argument may be 'hidden' – for example, a description of a disastrous aeroplane trip may imply an argument against air travel.

When reading these non-fiction texts, you need to show three things:
- that you understand what they are saying
- that you understand how and why they are written in the way they are
- that you have your own opinions about them.

The diagram below describes the reading skills that will be assessed in the assignment. On the left are the examiner's words; on the right that information is 'unpacked'.

'You will be assessed on your ability to distinguish between fact and opinion and evaluate how information is presented.'	• You need to show that you understand the point of view of each writer, and how all the points made in their texts back up that point of view. • You need to identify different techniques used in the arguments, and how the writer uses language and organises his/her ideas. • You also need to give your own opinion about the point of view and how it is presented.
'You will be assessed on your ability to select material appropriate to your purpose, collate material from different sources, and make cross references.'	• You need to show that you have understood what you have read by referring to features of the texts to support what you say. Sometimes this will involve bringing together features from several different texts (collating). • You will also have to compare at least two of the texts, making your references to the texts clear.

Note that you will not need to comment on the physical format or presentation of the non-fiction texts, as they will generally be presented as straight text documents.

The writing skills you will be assessed on

In the non-fiction section, you will also be given a writing task. This will relate in some way to the texts that you have been studying. You will be assessed on how well you can write to **inform**, to **explain** and to **describe**. Usually, the writing task will combine these three purposes in one piece of writing. The diagram below describes what writing skills will be assessed in the assignment. The examiner's words are on the left; on the right that information is 'unpacked'.

'You will be assessed on your ability to communicate clearly and imaginatively, using and adapting forms for different readers and purposes.'

→

- You need to think clearly about the purpose of the piece of writing, and who it is aimed at.
- Your writing should be adapted to this purpose and audience.
- Your vocabulary and style should be varied and effective.
- You need to think of some interesting and relevant ideas, and develop them through the piece.

'You will be assessed on your ability to organise ideas into sentences, paragraphs and whole texts, using a variety of linguistic and structural features.'

→

- You need to structure your text effectively. That means beginning and ending well, organising your points in paragraphs, and using presentational devices such as bullet points, if appropriate.
- Your sentences need to work together well.

'You will be assessed on your ability to use a range of sentence structures effectively with accurate punctuation and spelling.'

→

- You need to show that you can craft sentences in varied and effective ways, by using sentences of different kinds and different lengths. Do you need a short snappy sentence, for example? Or a longer, more descriptive or explanatory one?
- Marks are also awarded for correct grammar, punctuation and spelling.

Sample assignment on non-fiction texts

To help you understand what this section is leading up to this is what the second half of your assignment paper will look like. You should not tackle this assignment now as the full assignment, together with the texts, is given at the end of the Non-fiction section (pages 110–114). By the time you have studied this section in detail you will be ready to tackle the full assignment.

Remember

- You have 4 hours in total to complete all the tasks in the assignment. That includes the first half of the paper, on Media texts. So the Non-fiction questions should take approximately half that time.
- Note that the topics for the Media and Non-fiction texts are different from this book. In the actual Edexcel assessment the topic is the same for the Media and Non-fiction texts.
- In your actual assessment you will already have been studying the texts in the classroom for a few weeks before you are given the assignment.

The annotations show you what skills you need to learn, and where this book will help you to practise them.

> You need to be able to time yourself in the assignment room. 'Assignment tips' throughout the book give you practical help on how to tackle the assignment.

> You need to show that you understand the point of view of each writer, and how his or her arguments are constructed. (See pages 70–77.)

> You need to be able to spot any tricks or flaws in the arguments, and assess how well the writer has used techniques and language skills to get their point across. (See pages 78–86.)

> You need to be able to key in your final draft on a computer. 'Practise IT' boxes throughout the book give you practical help on how to improve your keying-in skills.

> You need to be able to write effectively to these three different purposes. The report will provide information (see pages 90–95 for writing to inform), explain the policy (see pages 95–101 for writing to explain) and describe it in some detail (see pages 102–108 for writing to describe).

TOGETHER OR APART?

You have a maximum of 4 hours to complete all the tasks below and on page 54.

You must study the following non-fiction texts (pages 116–9) in order to complete this task.

- 'The benefits of co-education'
- 'Girls and boys together'
- 'Are girls short-changed in the co-ed classroom?'
- 'What's good about single-sex schools?'

Stage 2: Analysing the arguments

You are a member of the school council. You have been asked to consider whether there should be more single-sex schools, as many people demand. You have been given some non-fiction texts to look at.

Task 3

Your task is to use the non-fiction texts in order to write an e-mail that outlines each side of the debate for the other school council members. In your e-mail you should:

- identify a number of arguments that put forward the two sides of the debate in the non-fiction texts
- show clearly how these non-fiction texts present their view of single sex schools.

You should write in continuous prose.

In this task you will be assessed for your reading skills.

(20 marks for Reading)

Stage 3: Reporting back

Task 4

You have now made your decision about the future of schools in your area. You have to write a report to the education committee, informing them of your decision, and explaining your reasons. You must describe one or two examples of excellent schools to back up your decision. These descriptions can be in the form of eyewitness reports.

You can decide either to make more schools single-sex, or to reduce the number of single-sex schools.

You will be assessed for your skills in writing to inform, explain, describe.

(20 marks for Writing)

The benefits of co-education

I'm not in any way against single-sex schools – it's more important that a school should be good. I favour co-education for the following reasons.

At some point in their lives boys and girls need to learn to work together. It's good preparation for the real world, and I don't agree that pupils at co-ed schools cannot attain the same academic standards.

From my own experience as an English teacher, you can teach English in a much more interesting way to a mixed class. You get more points of view, which make discussions all the more lively.

Girls in the Sixth Form at Loretto have been doing very well across the sciences, and particularly in physics. Many of them go on to study medicine.

Being co-ed provides Loretto with a ready-made community, which has considerable advantages in terms of activities like drama and music.

Many Lorettonians do the Gold Duke of Edinburgh Award. This gives boys and girls an opportunity to see how the others work under stress. Again, it's useful experience for the real world.

We held a charity concert for Tsunami Relief as well as a charity fashion show. These events show that boys and girls lead in different ways. It's perhaps a bit of a cliché, but boys tend to be more traditional in their approach and girls more radical. Clearly it's healthy for our senior pupils to learn the proper mix of these two approaches.

We have a seven-day week here, and boys and girls have busy lives with academic studies and all the activities. They also have social lives, and these have to be fitted in along with everything else. This teaches what I describe as the 'right sort of toughness'. Life at a co-ed school is more complex than a single-sex school but, I believe, more fun.

Families tend to be very busy, particularly if both parents work – many of our parents appreciate being able to send their sons and daughters to the same school. Logistically it has many advantages, but other benefits are the stability and sense of community that it gives, particularly for bigger families.

However, I'm all for choice and parents should be able to choose whether to send their children to a co-ed school or a single-sex school.

" Are girls short-changed in the co-ed classroom?

Research in both the UK and USA over the last 20 years has indicated that for many girls, a co-ed classroom does not help them to achieve equality, but indeed may depress self-confidence and limit aspirations. Many girls are short-changed by the co-ed classroom.

- **Boys dominate teacher time.** Classroom observations showed that boys answer and ask more questions, hog the teacher's attention and the apparatus, organise themselves more quickly and ruthlessly to their tasks, while girls hang back through shyness or a desire to be helpful and co-operative. Boys are more demanding of teachers' time both behaviourally and academically.

- **Girls are less likely to take intellectual risks and are more passive.** They fear getting it wrong, looking silly, being considered stupid, being judged by their male peers and found wanting. They prefer to solve problems by team working.

- **Subject choices are more likely to be polarised.** In co-ed schools both boys and girls are more likely to choose traditional male and female subjects. This limits choice and aspirations for both boys and girls.

- **Girls tend to lose self-esteem and confidence** as they progress through adolescence. This is made worse if they are constantly being placed under social pressure from boys. A co-ed environment does not always give them the space and security in which to build up their self-esteem and confidence in their own abilities as individuals.

- **Less positive role models for girls.** Co-ed schools do not always provide girls with the necessary positive role models through the teaching staff and the general ethos and philosophy of the school that is so essential for building girls' self-esteem and confidence. This is particularly the case for schools that have gone co-ed but where girls are in a minority. These are essentially still boys' schools with all the male traditions and trappings.

- **Girls mature physically, mentally and emotionally earlier than boys.** Girls and boys mature physically, mentally and emotionally at different ages. In a co-ed environment this is much more difficult to manage. Girls are likely to lose out, as they tend to mature earlier and may well be held back by slower developing boys.

- **Girls can have fewer opportunities for leadership roles** in co-ed schools. "

WHAT'S GOOD ABOUT SINGLE-SEX SCHOOLS?

Martin Hemming talks to teenagers about single sex education.

Are they missing out or having a ball?

Choosing between a single-sex or mixed school can create a dilemma for children and parents. Parents often feel their children will be able to work harder at a single-sex school with fewer distractions; but what do young people themselves say about single-sex schools? Are girls more confident of their abilities without boys around? Do boys concentrate more without girls to distract them?

Fleur

My primary school, like most, was mixed, so I thought that with all girls it would be a bit weird.

But now I prefer going to an all-girls school. With boys around I wouldn't be able to work as hard. My dad prefers it that there are no boys.

There's no one to impress at a girls' school. People come in and say: 'Oh, I just got out of bed.' But that's all right because there's nobody to look good for. You can look bad at school and when you go out you can show everyone how good you can look.

If we did have a mixed school, I think by Year 11 you'd be bored of the boys anyway. You'd have already been out with every single one of them!

Gordon

At an all-boys' school there are fewer distractions, I'd say. With girls around I think we'd be more mouthy to the teachers, trying to show off. At a boys' school you can act yourself. When you're in Year 7 you're just happy being with your mates. But when you start seeing your mates talking to girls you think, 'I've got to try that.' You just get interested and then addicted!

Jasmin

When I'm older, it's all going to depend on my education, so I'm just looking towards that really. I know I'll meet boys through the other stuff, like my youth club and the pantomime I'm in. You might not meet boys in secondary school, but you'll make friends with them at university or at work, so I wouldn't be too worried about it at the moment.

We have discos with boys' schools, but not many. But it's better like that. It makes you want to go to them more.

Yajnah

Being in an all-girls' school you can be with your friends more. Boys distract you. At a girls' school you can be closer to your friends, without being interrupted by boys. Although, just being girls, there are lots of arguments.

We have discos with the local boys' schools. I've been to some of them but I can't be bothered with them any more. Meeting boys isn't really the most important thing right now.

Girls and boys together

Proponents of co-education point to powerful pressures that encourage educating girls and boys under the same roof. Simple logistics in a busy world make schooling sons and daughters together attractive.

'Co-ed schools accord with parents' demands – it's easier to have all the family's children at school in one place,' said Jean Hall, founder of a management consultancy that has helped a number of schools embrace the change. 'Working mums and dads don't have time to liaise with different schools.'

Mixed schools are also the norm in the British state sector: the single-sex institutions largely disappeared in the 1960s and 1970s when they were merged to form comprehensives. Out of 3000 state secondary schools, just 184 cater only for boys and 226 for girls.

Like others, Hall also argues that co-education is the best preparation for a 'co-educational' world. 'It provides preparation for life after school, including the workplace,' she said.

Some parents believe it helps girls and boys learn to understand each other early on, rather than being suddenly flung together at university.

David Pierce, 19, and now at Hull University, attended first a boys' school then a co-ed. 'At a single-sex school you don't get to hear about girls' problems: you have less knowledge about them,' he said. 'You wouldn't be able to talk to girls on a friendly basis, you wouldn't have as much experience of talking to girls.'

Katie Banks, 23, and now working at a media firm in London as an intern, went to a girls-only school and said: 'There was a lack of banter in the classroom – boys bring a different perspective. And then you suddenly get launched into university and it's a bit like a sweetshop. You weren't used to seeing boys as friends – they were potential boyfriends.'

Despite those drawbacks, however, Pierce found that single-sex schools had one distinct advantage. He preferred it for sport because in a co-ed school 'girls could always run faster than me, which was a major embarrassment'.

D Reading non-fiction texts

Reading an argument

> ### My learning
>
> In 'Reading an argument' I will:
> • learn what an argument is
> • identify an author's point of view
> • summarise the key points in an argument

Non-fiction texts often include arguments. For example, a newspaper column may argue that young people spend too much time playing computer games. Or a political leaflet may argue that you should vote for a particular party.

An argument is a structured way of putting forward a point of view. The aim or **purpose** is to persuade the reader to agree with that point of view (P.O.V.).

Identifying a point of view

The point of view is the main message that the arguer is trying to get across. That message is usually backed up by other points, such as reasons or examples. But identifying the point of view is the first important step in understanding an argument.

Activity 1

1 Read the extract on page 70, from a letter to a teen magazine.

2 The author's purpose is to argue for a particular point of view. Which of these statements describes the point of view?
   a) It's not healthy to surround yourself with members of one sex only.
   b) Most people meet their life partners at school or college.
   c) Single-sex schools are not a good idea.

3 Identify at least two other points that back up the writer's point of view.

> ## SINGLE SEX = NO FUN!
>
> Single-sex schools? You must be joking! It's definitely unhealthy to surround yourself with all boys or all girls. How would you meet people that you might marry? Most people get married because they met at school or college. Single-sex schools just don't prepare you for the real world. And they're no fun either!
>
> **Jamie, 14, Nottingham**

Following an argument

Once you have identified the author's point of view, you need to look more closely at the steps that lead there. These steps are the key points of the argument. If the text is well written, then each paragraph is likely to contain a different point. You can use the paragraphing to help you identify the steps in the argument.

Activity 2

1 Read the text on page 71. It is an extract from a book aimed at teenage boys. The author's point of view in this extract is that conversation is really important when hitting it off with girls.

2 Working with a partner, identify the steps (main points) in the argument. Use the paragraphs to help you.

3 Summarise each step. Use a graphic like the one started below.

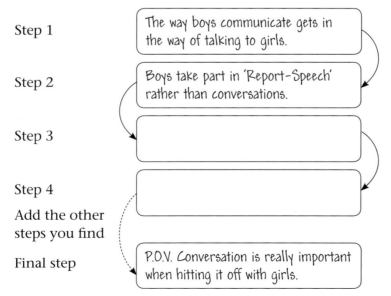

Step 1 — The way boys communicate gets in the way of talking to girls.

Step 2 — Boys take part in 'Report-Speech' rather than conversations.

Step 3 —

Step 4 —

Add the other steps you find

Final step — P.O.V. Conversation is really important when hitting it off with girls.

Assignment tip

As you study your non-fiction texts, draw up a table listing the important things about each argument. Focus on:
- point of view (purpose)
- key points
- audience.

This will prepare you well for any question in the assignment.

Communication skills

The way that boys learn to communicate with each other isn't necessarily much help when it comes to communicating with girls. In fact, it can actually be a handicap.

A lot of the time boys don't have what you might call conversations. It's sort of Report-Speech. 'I'll report something funny/scary/unusual that I've seen, heard or thought of and then you tell *me* something.'

The aim is to *impress* each other or whoever else is listening. The responses to 'impressive' statements may well include 'Wow', 'Really?' or 'You're a lying toad'. But they don't necessarily go much deeper, and they don't by any means always develop into a proper conversation.

Striking up a friendship with a girl involves using communication skills which a lot of boys have never learnt, mainly because they've never had to. Their previous friendships have been with members of their own sex where actual *conversation* has never really taken place.

Because a lot of boys rarely talk to each other about anything that is deeply personal they are not well trained in the art of conversation. They are not used to describing their emotions or feelings to one another, nor are they practised at just opening up and being vulnerable.

Often they don't have much of a handle on small-talk or chit-chat either, because it doesn't exist within their world of Report-Speech and impressive tales.

In fact they're often much happier doing something that is a focus in itself, rather than having to find a topic for discussion.

On the contrary, girls' friendships seem to function in a different way. They spend a lot less time *doing* things and more time talking about things.

What is actually more important is to make contact, to create some communication which stems from sharing a conversation, not giving a gut-bustin', one-sided, stand-up performance. Indeed when starting a friendship with any girl, the greatest asset a boy can have is not a quick, witty tongue, but an attentive ear .

Conversation is the key, it's the starting point of any relationship with the opposite sex. That doesn't mean it can only be practised on members of the opposite sex, far from it; the 'art of conversation', the ability to speak interestingly, listen attentively and identify similar thoughts, feelings and experiences, can and should be perfected by talking with anyone and everyone.

N. Fisher, *Boys about Boys*

Thinking about the audience

So far you have been focusing on the purpose of an argument text – to get a point of view across. Thinking about the audience is also key to 'reading' a text. Just like any other text, an argument needs to use the right language and presentation to suit the audience it is aiming at.

Activity 3

1 What audience is the author of 'Communication skills' (see page 71) aiming at?

2 Look at each of the following features of the text. Write some notes to comment on how well the author has adapted his writing to take the audience into account. Give him a mark out of 10 in each case. An example has been given to start you off (which may not be your own view!).

- **Vocabulary.** What kind of words are used? – *Sometimes words are used to appeal directly to the audience, e.g. 'gut-bustin', 'small-talk'. Sometimes the opposite – there are words that a young teenage boy would not be used to, like 'vulnerable' or 'attentively'. In general, the vocabulary is somewhere in the middle.* **5/10**
- **Formality.** How (in)formal are the words? How (in)formally are the ideas presented?
- **Sentences.** How long? Different types?
- **Structure.** Clear structure of ideas? Use/length of paragraphs?
- **Relationship to audience.** Tone? Talking down? On same level? Addressing them directly?

3 Share your notes and marks with a partner. Come up with a joint view on how well you think the author has taken the audience into account. If you have given the author low marks, write down the most important thing you think he should do differently.

Assignment tip

You often need to summarise the main points of a text. Make sure you do not copy out whole sentences. Summarising means identifying the key things, so only the essential detail is needed. Using your own words in your summary shows that you really understand what the author is saying, who the writer is trying to reach, and why.

Practise IT

Printing
Sharing notes with others can be easier if you have a printed copy (or two). To print off a copy of your work first click on File at the top of the screen and then select Print. In the pop-up box, choose the number of copies you want and then click on OK.

Key points

- An argument is a structured way of putting forward a point of view. Its purpose is to persuade the reader to agree with that point of view.
- Identifying the point of view is the first important step in understanding an argument.
- Summarise the key points of the argument in your own words. Use the way the text is divided into paragraphs to help you.
- Arguments take account of their audience, just like other types of text. Vocabulary, sentences, structure, formality and tone should all be appropriate to the audience.

Speaking and listening

Speaking and listening opportunity

AO1(iii) Adopt roles and communicate with audiences using a range of techniques
This is a *drama-focused* activity. It will be used to assess how well you can *explore/analyse/imagine.*

In groups of four, your task is to improvise a short sketch to show the rest of the class how boys and girls communicate.

1 Explore the ideas in the extract 'Communication skills' (page 71).
2 Agree on a general approach.
  - Will you role-play a pair of boys, then a pair of girls? Or cut backwards and forwards between them?
  - Will you show a difference in the ways that boys and girls communicate?
  - Will you include a 'boy meets girl' scene?
  - Will you address the audience?
  - Will your sketch be funny or serious?
3 Discuss the detail of the role-play. Then improvise the sketch.

> *To gain good marks you need to:*
> – *keep a role going effectively, engaging the audience's interest*
> – *use different dramatic techniques to do this*
> – *show that you really understand the issues behind the role-play*
> – *show that you have some good ideas, and that you can use drama to communicate those ideas.*

Analysing an argument

My learning

In 'Analysing an argument' I will:
- explore the different kinds of reasons or evidence that make up an argument
- analyse an argument by identifying the techniques used.

Identifying the techniques

To analyse an argument (that is, to break it down into its different parts and say how it works) you need to do more than identify the key points. You also need to say what techniques it is using. The techniques are the different kinds of reasoning used to back up the main point of view.

The argument tree below describes some of these common techniques. The main point of the argument is the trunk. The branches represent different ways in which the conclusion can be backed up.

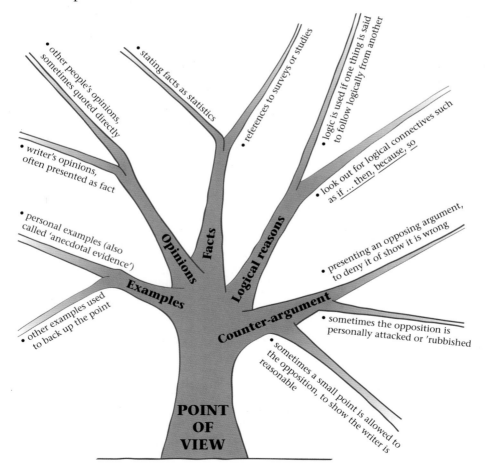

- other people's opinions, sometimes quoted directly
- stating facts as statistics
- references to surveys or studies
- logic is used if one thing is said to follow logically from another
- writer's opinions, often presented as fact
- look out for logical connectives such as if … then, because, so
- personal examples (also called 'anecdotal evidence')
- presenting an opposing argument, to deny it of show it is wrong
- other examples used to back up the point
- sometimes the opposition is personally attacked or 'rubbished
- sometimes a small point is allowed to the opposition, to show the writer is reasonable

Opinions

Facts

Logical reasons

Examples

Counter-argument

POINT OF VIEW

Activity 4

1 Read the newspaper article 'Hit or myth' (below), which examines some myths about women.

2 Each numbered point uses one of the techniques described in the argument tree on page 74. Identify which one is being used, and match it with one of the descriptions (A to I) on page 76.

3 Write a comment about how effective you think each point is in backing up the author's point of view.

Hit or myth ... is there any truth in all those tales about women?

Do blondes really have more fun? Are women hopeless at driving and reading maps? Do they talk too much? We decided to investigate.

Women are bad drivers

This old chestnut is rolled out virtually every time a woman gets into the driving seat and a (usually grudging) male passenger sits beside her. But if **1** true, why do motor insurance companies offer women more competitive rates? The indisputable facts are: women have **2** better claims records than men and far fewer motoring convictions.

When road safety organisation Brake **3** surveyed 1000 motorists, far more men than women admitted speeding. Females **4** are half as likely as men to risk driving the morning after they have drunk heavily – 11% compared to 22%. Finally, the AA **5** reports that women don't feel the need to impress other drivers or passengers with Michael Schumacher-style antics.

Verdict: False

Women take ages getting ready

Women takes ages preparing for a night **6** out? If only. Admittedly, teenage girls do take their time, but as responsibilities multiply with the years, so the luxury of time to pamper yourself disappears. It's a tragedy but there it is.

Just as women with babies eat faster than **7** anyone else (stuffing in as much nutrition as possible before some crisis erupts), so women with men and children in tow refine their getting ready ritual to a quick-change routine, a dab of scent, a once over with the lippie and a search for those earrings you left in a saucer in the kitchen. Ten minutes max. Then you sit in the car drumming your (regretfully unmanicured) fingers on the wheel while your husband follows his obsessive leaving the house procedure and cleans his shoes.

This is the true picture, unpalatable as it **8** may be to men who like to perpetrate the **9** nonsense that women (a) have no sense of time and (b) cannot tear themselves away from the mirror.

Verdict: False

Daily Express, 5 December 2003

A A minor **counter-argument** is allowed, to show the writer is reasonable.
B The writer gives own **opinion**.
C The **opinion** of an organisation is reported.
D The writer gives precise **statistics** to back up the argument.
E The opposition (**counter-argument**) is rubbished.
F Some basic **facts** are stated.
G Results of a **survey** are given.
H The writer uses **logic** – one thing follows logically from another.
I The writer gives a lengthy **example** describing what really happens.

Activity 5

1 Read the press release below, which was issued by the Fawcett Society, a pressure group for women's rights. It was published in response to comments by newsreader Michael Buerk that women are too powerful in society. You will have the opportunity to analyse Michael Buerk's comments later in this section on page 82.

2 Note down:
   a) the point of view of this argument
   b) three different ways in which the argument is backed up.

If you need help, refer to the argument tree on page 75.

Fawcett responds to Michael Buerk: news release, 16 August 2005

Just a simple look at the facts shows that we do not yet have equality between the sexes in the UK, never mind the notion that women now hold more power than men.

Women are still paid less than men and too few women are still not reaching the top in the media, business, public life or politics in anything like the numbers that men are.

It is true that we have had a revolution in women's lives over the past 30 years. But our long-hours working culture still means that women, who are much more likely to have caring responsibilities, find it impossible to compete on an equal basis with men in the workplace. In the home, domestic chores are still not shared equally, even when a couple both work full time.

We now need a revolution in men's lives too – a total rethink of the way that home life and work life are organised for women and men. Indeed, many men welcome the fact that stereotypes of what are suitable roles for each sex are slowly being broken down, allowing them to do things such as spend more time with their children.

Many men support our campaign for a society in which women and men are equal partners at work, at home and in public life.

Useful facts
- There is still an hourly pay gap between women and men of nearly 20% for full-time work and 40% for part-time work.
- Just 20% of our MPs are women.
- Just 2% of executive directors of our top 100 companies are women.
- Only around 15% of UK national newspapers have a woman editor.
- Of the 12 judges in the House of Lords – the highest court in the land – there is only one woman.

Key points

- Analysing an argument means identifying the techniques used to back up a point of view.
- Points of view can be backed up by using examples, opinions, facts, logic and counter-arguments.

The language of arguments

My learning

In 'The language of argument' I will:
* investigate different language effects that can add power to an argument
* think about how language can bias an argument in a writer's favour.

Looking at language

Rather like a joke, the impact of an argument is improved if it is delivered well. That means using language effectively.

As a reader of non-fiction texts, you need to show that you can recognise exactly how the language of an argument contributes to its power.

Language effects are often called rhetorical techniques. Their aim is to get the audience on your side. Here are some common examples.
* **Personal pronouns** (e.g. *I*, *you* and *we*) add a personal touch.
* **Rhetorical questions** – questions asked for effect, not for an answer.
* **Effective words** – colourful and powerful nouns, verbs and adjectives.
* **Sound effects**, such as alliteration (e.g. *terrible twins*) and onomatopoeia (same vowel sounds, e.g. *free speech*), repetition and rhyming.
* **Sentence skills** – varying the type and length of sentence for effect.

Assignment tip

Remember the mnemonic **PRESS**. It gives you the first letter of each of the five rhetorical effects listed opposite.

Activity 6

The newspaper article on page 78 is a contribution to the debate about whether men should cry. (The debate was inspired by a report that Claudio Ranieri, then manager of Chelsea, had wept when he heard of his team's victory over Arsenal.)

1 Read the article. The notes on the first half highlight how the author has used language effectively to make his argument more persuasive.

2 Identify at least four more rhetorical techniques in the rest of the article. Note down what makes them effective.

Rhetorical question – a question asked for effect, not for an answer.

Varying the length of the sentences for effect. 'All was silent' reflects the stillness.

Repetition of 'an instant, to emphasise how quickly one thing followed another.

Powerful verbs – 'weeping' (rather than crying) and 'cracking'.

Complex and well-constructed sentence.

Repetition of d and s sounds (alliteration) and of solemn long vowel sound (assonance).

Use of pronoun 'I' throughout – makes argument personal.

Almost poetic language, to make the old soldiers sound more heroic.

There is nothing unmanly about tears

Bruce Anderson, political columnist

Sunt lacrimae rerum; does any language offer such profundity in three words? They are untranslatable but, with apologies to Virgil, one free approximation might be: 'At moments the human condition calls for tears.'

So it does, even on dubious occasions. After Robert Kennedy's assassination, a large crowd watched his coffin pass the Washington Monument at a slow march. All was silent. Then someone started to sing the Battle Hymn of the Republic in a low voice.

An instant later, everyone was singing. An instant after that, even the National Guardsmen were weeping. Though I believe Bobby Kennedy's death saved America from a bad presidency, I cannot tell that story without my voice cracking and my eyes watering.

In 1984, at the Tory party conference, Michael Heseltine talked about the D-Day celebration earlier that year. Forty years on, as he described it, the veterans may have been less robust in wind and limb, but as they paraded, all that was forgotten.

For a moment, ageing ceased and heroism returned. By the time Heseltine had finished, there was not a dry eye in the house: certainly not mine. Afterwards I taxed him with being a cynical old so-and-so who had manipulated his audience's emotions. He indignantly denied it. They were his own emotions, and his only problem had been to deliver the speech without breaking down. At the celebrations, he had wept copiously. But, as he said: 'I cry easily.'

So did Churchill. There is nothing unmanly or self-indulgent about tears. I defy anyone to remain dry-eyed in the cemeteries of Flanders, or in a little graveyard at San Carlos Water, in the Falklands. It is the final parade ground for Lt-Col H Jones, VC, and 12 of his comrades. I am sure mine are not the only eyes which have watered that green grass.

Leaving aside the agonies of despair, men weep most naturally when they are moved by great deeds, either in real life or in the world of imagination.

When the play *All's Well That Ends Well* is moving to a happy ending, the good Lord Lafew says: 'Mine eyes smell onions, I shall weep anon.' On Tuesday, Claudio Ranieri smelt onions. Why not?

Independent, 8 April 2004

Assessing emotive language

Some words are so powerful that they create strong feelings in an audience. We call this emotive language. When reading an argument that is expressed in emotive language, you need to ask whether the language is so strong that it unfairly biases the reader in favour of the writer's view.

Activity 7

The emotive language in the paragraph below has been highlighted.

1 Discuss with a partner what the writer wants the reader to feel in each case.

2 Discuss whether you think the language is so strong that it unfairly biases the argument.

3 Make notes on the results of your discussion, to be shared in class.

Assignment tip

You have to decide whether language effects, especially emotive language, are unfair. That means looking 'beneath' the language to assess the quality of the argument.

Testosterone is the hormone of success and competitiveness. But testosterone-fuelled boys and young men are potentially a lethal weapon. Most parents are aware of the almost insatiable desire that their sons have to watch violent films, and how they have to be dragged away from the computer, where they have been indulging in *Manhunt II* and other appalling games …

Activity 8

1 Read another contribution to the 'Men don't cry' debate (see page 80).

2 Prepare a short presentation to explain how Terence Blacker uses language to make his argument more effective. Organise your presentation around the rhetorical techniques listed on page 77.

3 State in your presentation whether you think the argument is biased because of any emotive language used, giving examples.

It's unattractive and undignified

Terence Blacker, author

Frankly, I'm embarrassed by how damp-eyed and trembly lipped men have recently become. It is an unattractive and undignified trend and it is time for us all to snap out of it. I should confess that I can well up at the slightest excuse – winning, losing, loving, the sound of children, virtually any film, 'St Matthew's Passion', a couple of routines from the show *Anything Goes* – but at least I have the decency to be ashamed of myself and try to do it alone or in the dark.

It's true that, unlike women, at least most men don't cry to win arguments or gain sympathy (yet) but there is something indulgent about male tears, an unhealthy luxuriating in emotion and self-pity.

But, if for a man to cry in private is embarrassing, doing it in public is far worse. Think of Billy Connolly weeping during Live Aid, Roger Federer wailing like a baby after Wimbledon, the various Oscar-winning idiots in Hollywood. The more a politician cries, the less he is to be trusted. Both Bushes were in tears at Junior's inauguration ceremony and there has been much White House blubbing – caused by the death of Americans or of the president's dog – since then.

'Look how sensitive I am,' these public tears are saying. 'I'm a caring, vulnerable guy in touch with my feelings.' It is the worst kind of emotional flashing. Handkerchiefs away, chaps. It's time for manliness to make a comeback.

The Independant 8 April 2004

Key points

- Language can be used to back up the force of an argument.
- Effective arguments often include rhetorical techniques: personal pronouns, rhetorical questions, effective words, sound effects and sentence skills (**PRESS**).
- You have to judge whether language effects, especially emotive language, unfairly bias the reader in favour of the argument.

Tricks and flaws in arguments

My learning

In 'Tricks and flaws in arguments' I will:
- *learn about the dirty tricks and errors that arguments sometimes contain*
- *practise identifying these tricks and flaws, using the correct terms.*

Sometimes arguments use underhand methods to make their point. If these are deliberate, you could call them dirty tricks. Often, though, they are simply errors (or 'flaws'). When you read an argument, you need to be on the lookout for tricks or flaws.

Assignment tip

When you write about arguments in the exam, try to use some of the terms that relate to the techniques, tricks or errors that you notice, e.g. *flaw, reason, opinion, generalisation, selective evidence, irrelevance*. Using the correct technical term will help you to make a focused point, and will show the examiner that you know what you are talking about.

Activity 9

1 Read extracts 1 to 8, which come from letters to a newspaper responding to a story claiming that exam results showed yet again that girls are cleverer than boys.

2 The speech bubbles comment on the tricks and flaws that the arguments contain. Working with a partner, match each letter with the correct speech bubble.

1 Girls cleverer than boys? Both I and my two best friends ended up with 4 good A levels at school. No, none of us is female.

A This is a huge **exaggeration**. The statements about boys and the language used are over the top. This undermines the argument.

2 Men are risk-takers who think outside the box. They are very individualistic, unlike women who need to conform. As boys, at school, they just aren't interested in getting good grades.

B This is just **personal** (or 'anecdotal') **evidence**. Referring to your own experience may help to back up an argument, but on its own it is not enough.

3 I'm not surprised that boys are falling behind. Any teacher of teens will tell you that boys think (a) being thick/criminal/aggressive is cool, and (b) the world owes them a salary and lifestyle equivalent to that of a professional footballer, with little or no effort on their part.

C This is **selective evidence** – the evidence mentioned is very narrow. Here only science is mentioned, and science at the highest levels.

D This reference to co-ed schools is **irrelevant**. The quality of co-educational schools is not the subject of the argument. Irrelevance is a flaw in the argument.

4 It's another attempt to do men down. Ever since primary school they are put down by women teachers, then told off by their mothers at home. Exams are set by women and marked by women. Even your report was written by a woman. Nuff said.

E This is simply **inconsistent**. What the writer says about science in the first part of the argument doesn't fit with what she says at the end. This is a logical flaw in the argument.

5 The rise in girl gangs and 'ladette' culture shows that girls won't be on top for very long. Soon they will be down at the boys' level again.

F This is **over-generalising** – drawing a big conclusion from a small piece of evidence. An observation about the behaviour of a few girls has been used to suggest that all girls will soon follow suit. This is a flaw in the argument.

6 Women overtaking men? The Internet revolution was conceived of, designed and implemented by men. Out of 300 scientific Nobel prizes in history, only about 10 went to women. The ratio hasn't changed.

G This is just **stating an opinion as a fact**. The writer is making an interesting statement about how men think, but it is still just his opinion. It can't be proved, and it isn't backed up by further evidence.

7 Students who go to co-ed schools get just as good results as any others. Girls and boys are treated as equals, and they come out with equal honours in exams.

8 Girls may get better results overall, but in science they are still flagging behind boys, especially in co-ed schools. Boys are just as good as girls at science, and always will be.

H This is just **abusing the opposition**. There's the glimmer of an interesting point here, but it's lost among the general abuse of women. When a writer addresses the opposition rather than the facts, you need to ask if this is relevant to the argument.

Activity 10

1 Read the newspaper article below, which reports an argument about the sex war.

2 Identify at least two tricks or flaws in newsreader Michael Buerk's argument. Explain why each one undermines the argument. Quote from the article in your answer, and use the technical terms highlighted in the bubbles on page 81.

'Life is now lived by women's rules,' says Buerk

Craig Brown

MICHAEL Buerk, the BBC newsreader, has complained that the 'shift in the balance of power between the sexes' has gone too far, and that 'life is now lived in accordance with women's rules'.

Citing the number of females in the top jobs in BBC broadcasting as an example, he has claimed that 'these are the people who decide what we see and hear'.

Buerk, who complains that men have been reduced to 'sperm donors', told the *Radio Times* magazine that society needs to admit there is a problem.

'Life is now being lived according to women's rules,' he said.

'The traits that have traditionally been associated with men – reticence, stoicism, single-mindedness – have been marginalised.

'The result is that men are becoming more like women. Look at the men who are being held up as sporting icons – David Beckham and, God forbid, Tim Henman.'

Buerk added: 'Look at the changes in the workplace. There is no manufacturing industry any more; there are no mines; few vital jobs require physical strength.

'What we have now are lots of jobs that require people skills and multi-tasking – which women are a lot better at.'

Buerk, whose views will also be screened this week in 'Don't Get Me Started!', a Channel Five series on personal hobbyhorses, said

that when he started making the programme he 'came across what I considered a very personal example of the changes that have taken place.

'Almost all the big jobs in broadcasting were held by women – the controllers of BBC1 television and Radio 4 for example. These are the people who decide what we see and hear.'

BBC1 Controller Lorraine Heggessey has since left the BBC and been replaced by a man, Peter Fincham, while Radio 4 is still run by Janice Hadlow.

The Scotsman 16 August 2005

Key points

- Look out for any tricks or flaws in arguments that you read or hear.
- Common tricks and flaws are: anecdotal evidence, opinions presented as facts, exaggeration, abusing the opposition, over-generalising, selecting the evidence, irrelevance and inconsistency.

Evaluating arguments

My learning

In 'Evaluating arguments' I will:
- learn what evaluating an argument means
- use all the knowledge that I have built up so far to evaluate a complete argument.

Arguing with the arguer

Here is an argument about single-sex education:

> *Boys mature later than girls. Therefore they should be educated separately from girls.*

The point of view is clear – boys should be educated separately from girls (note the connective *therefore*). The reason given is also clear – this is because boys mature later than girls. However, you might want to challenge this argument in various different ways. For example:

Assignment tip

You may be asked in the assignment not only to outline the main points in an argument, but also to evaluate it. To practise this skill, try questioning any argument that you read or hear. Don't take any argument for granted – there is usually something you can say on the other side, or a question you could ask.

Boys reach puberty later than girls, but why does that mean they should be educated separately? More evidence is needed to reach this conclusion.

Single-sex schools also have disadvantages. These aren't mentioned, but they might outweigh the advantages.

This isn't the only conclusion to follow from the evidence. You could argue instead that teachers should allow for the different maturity rates of boys and girls. It is a big leap to say that they have to be taught separately.

Speaking and listening opportunity

AO1(ii) *Participate in discussion by both speaking and listening. Judge the nature and purposes of contributions and the roles of participants*
This is a ***discussion-based*** activity. It will be used to assess how well you can ***discuss/argue/persuade***.

1 In small groups, discuss what objections, challenges or questions you can come up with in response to the following argument.
Boys and girls have to get on together in the outside world. Therefore it makes sense for them to be educated together in co-educational schools.
2 Record the results of your discussion. Note down each challenge, and who makes the challenge.
3 Appoint a spokesperson to feed back the results to the class.

To gain good marks you need to:
– *play a leading part in the discussion*
– *make good contributions that are well-expressed*
– *listen sensitively, and show that you can work well as part of a group*
– *challenge constructively, building on points made by others.*

Evaluating an argument

When you evaluate something, you say how effective it is overall, quoting examples and giving reasons. So evaluating an argument means using your knowledge of all the techniques used by the writer, plus your own challenges and thoughts about the argument.

Activity 10

1 Read 'Our Biology Hasn't Changed Much' on page 85. It comes from an international bestseller written by two writers who describe themselves as 'experts in human relations and body language'.

2 With a partner, draw up and complete a table like the one below to help you evaluate the argument.

Main points of the argument	What technique is being used? (e.g. fact, opinion, example, logic, counter-argument – see page 74)	Are there any language effects? (Remember PRESS – see page 77)	Is it a trick or a flaw? (See page 81)	Any comments of your own?
Point 1 (para. 1) Boys and girls are different cos of their different interests.	This is the point of view – stated at the start.	Skilful writing of opening two sentences, clearly contrasting boys and girls. Short final sentence for effect.	Perhaps over-generalising in listing the different interests.	I know lots of boys who are interested in people!
Point 2 (para 2) How kibbutzim in Israel have tried to show that differences are really stereotyping.	The main example used to prove the conclusion. (This is actually a counter-argument, which is then knocked down.)	Long lists used to emphasise the efforts made.		
Point 3 (para 3) The aim of kibbutzim – sexually neutral society and equal opportunity.				
Point 4 (para 4) Studies show that these aims failed.				
Point 5 (para 5) Studies show that sex differences can't be reduced.				
Conclusion				

Our Biology Hasn't Changed Much

Boys want to play with things; girls want to interact with people. Boys want to control, dominate and reach the top, but girls are more concerned with morality, relationships and people. Women are still a minority in big business and the political arena, but not because of male oppression. It's just that women are not interested in those things.

Israeli kibbutzim[1] have for years tried to remove the sex stereotyping of boys and girls. Children's clothes, shoes, hairstyles and lifestyles were fashioned on one sexless, neutral model. Boys were encouraged to play with dolls, sew, knit, cook and clean, and girls were motivated to play football, climb trees and play darts.

The idea of the kibbutz was to have a sexually neutral society in which there were no rigid formulae for each sex, and each member had equal opportunity and equal responsibility within the group. Sexist language and phrases like 'big boys don't cry' and 'little girls don't play in the dirt' were removed from the language and kibbutzniks claimed that they could demonstrate a complete interchangeability of roles between the sexes. So, what happened?

After 90 years of kibbutzim, studies have shown that boys in the kibbutz constantly display aggressive and disobedient behaviour, form power groups, fight amongst themselves, form unwritten hierarchies and do 'deals', while girls co-operate with each other, avoid conflicts, act affectionately, make friends and share with one another. Given a free hand to choose their own school courses and subjects, each opted for sex-specific courses, with boys studying physics, engineering and sports, and girls becoming teachers, counsellors, nurses and personnel managers. Their biology directed them to pursuits and occupations that fitted the wiring of their brains.

Studies of neutrally reared children in these societies show the removal of the mother/child bond does not reduce the sex differences or preferences in children. Rather, it creates a generation of children who feel neglected and confused and are likely to grow into screwed-up adults.

[1]A kibbutz (plural: kibbutzim) is a rural settlement in Israel. The land is owned by all its members in common, and children are reared collectively.

Allan and Barbara Pease, *Why Men Don't Listen and Women Can't Read Maps*

Assignment tip

As you study your non-fiction assignment texts, it's a good idea to draw up a table for each argument, like the one on page 85. It will focus your thoughts, and will act as a useful revision guide when it comes to the actual assignment. Remember that you cannot take notes like this into the assessment room.

Activity 11

On your own, use the notes in your table to write an evaluation of the argument 'Our Biology Hasn't Changed Much' in continuous prose. You need to organise your writing in three sections.

1 A statement of what the **purpose** of the argument is.

2 A list of the **key points**, commenting on each one in turn. You should comment on:
   - what part each point plays in the argument overall
   - any effective use of language
   - any trick or flaw that undermines the argument.
   Add any thoughts or challenges of your own.

3 A **conclusion**, summarising what you think about the argument.

Key points

- Evaluating an argument means using your knowledge of all the techniques used by the writer, plus your own challenges and thoughts about the argument, to assess how effective it is overall.
- Practise questioning and challenging any argument that you read or hear.

Quoting and comparing

My learning

In 'Quoting and comparing' I will:
- learn how to quote effectively from texts to make a point
- learn how to compare different points of view.

Quoting

You often need to quote from a text to back up a point that you are making. Note these key points about using quotations.
- Only quote in full when the actual words of the original are important to the point you are making.
- Remember to use inverted commas to show quoted material.
- Using your own words, instead of quoting, shows that you have understood what the text means.

Activity 12

1 Read what one student says (below) about the opening of the article 'Battle of the Sexes' on page 88.

2 Identify where she has followed the three pieces of advice above.

3 Discuss with a partner one or two points that you could make about the rest of the 'Battle of the Sexes' text.

4 On your own, choose one of these points and write it down. Quote the key words or phrases to back up your point.

A bald factual statement grabs the reader's attention right from the start: 'Men are by far the more violent sex.' The question and answer that follow raise a possible counter-argument ('an unfair prejudice?'), only to dash it immediately in the next sentence. The final sentence gives the reason why the controversial statement at the start is indeed fact – the 'statistics on aggression' prove it.

Battle of the Sexes

Men are by far the more violent sex. An unfair prejudice? No, a statement of fact. A glance through the statistics on aggression confirms that when it comes to a fight, men and women really are worlds apart.

Boys battle

Even as tiny tots the patterns are set. From two years old upward, males display aggression more often than females – and across all cultures. Continuing into adulthood, sex differences in aggression remain a human universal.

In 1989, Professor Rita Simon and colleagues from the Department of Justice, Law and Society at the American University in Washington DC, assessed the role of gender in violent crime. The study looked at homicide rates in 31 countries across a time span of 18 years and found no time or country in which female aggression exceeded that of male aggression.

Comparing texts

Sometimes you will be asked to compare two or more texts. This means discussing the similarities and differences between them. Follow these guidelines.

• Begin by comparing the purpose and audience of the texts.
• You could discuss Text 1 and then Text 2, and sum up at the end. This approach is straightforward, but it doesn't allow you to compare them side by side in detail.
• It is more effective to take a point at a time and compare both texts at once. Begin a new paragraph each time you start a different point.
• 'Signpost' clearly for the reader which text you are talking about. Use words such as such as 'both', 'also' and 'similarly' to show you are talking about similarities. Use words such as 'by contrast', 'however' and 'but' to indicate differences.
• The comparison need not only be factual. Include your own evaluation of the texts. You can sum up your evaluation in a concluding paragraph.

Assignment tip

Don't rely on a spellchecker to do all your checking for you in the exam. Spellcheckers only check spelling, not whether you have used effective words, or put them in the best order. They also only check that the word you type actually exists as a word – it may be the wrong form of the word (e.g. 'says' instead of 'said'), or even a completely different word from the one you want (e.g. 'rote' instead of 'wrote'). There is no substitute for carefully reading through your work, checking for places where you can improve the wording, grammar, punctuation and spelling.

Activity 13

1 On page 89, read how one student has begun a comparison of the two arguments about men crying (see the articles on pages 78 and 80)

2 The eight notes around the essay help you to see how the student has followed the advice above. Answer the question that follows each note.

1 The first paragraph discusses the purpose and audience of both texts. Why does the student do this?

3 Putting the writers' names first in the sentence makes it clear who you are talking about. Where else does the student do this?

5 The word 'both' shows you that you are writing about a *similarity* between the texts. Where else has the student signalled a similarity?

7 The student gives his own opinion about the texts. It isn't just a factual comparison. Where else does he give his opinion?

Both arguments are written for the same audience, as they are contributions to a debate in a national newspaper. However, they have completely different purposes. Terence Blacker's aim is to persuade us that it is 'unattractive and undignified' for men to cry; Bruce Anderson, by contrast, argues that there is 'nothing unmanly' about tears.

Terence Blacker begins by admitting that he is tempted to cry at all sorts of occasions. This is quite a clever move on his part, as it immediately gets us on his side – he isn't pretending to be a dry-eyed macho type. However, you could argue that this undermines his case from the start: if even Blacker cries, why shouldn't it be regarded as perfectly natural? Bruce Anderson, for example, is quite open about his own tears (his eyes are 'watering' throughout his article). Yet this leads him to the opposite conclusion – that it's fine for men to cry.

Blacker states in the second paragraph that there is 'something indulgent' about male tears, but he doesn't back this opinion up. Bruce Anderson says the opposite: 'There is nothing unmanly or self-indulgent about tears', but he backs it up by giving an example of how crying at war graves is a natural reaction.

Both writers use powerful words and images to make their arguments more effective. Blacker, for example, uses the words 'luxuriating' and 'blubbing', and the image of 'emotional flashing'. Anderson tends to use rather poetic clichés, such as 'watered that green grass' and 'less robust in wind and limb'. He also uses quotations from literature at the beginning and end of the article, which I find a bit pretentious.

2 This phrase signals to the reader that a difference is being commented on. Where else does the student do this?

4 This paragraph compares how the two writers refer to their own experiences of crying. What two points are being compared in the next two paragraphs?

6 The student quotes effectively from the texts. Where else does he do this?

8 These texts have been compared side by side throughout the essay. How effective would the comparison have been if the student had discussed each text in turn?

Key point

- Only quote in full when the actual words of the original are important to the point you are making. Using your own words shows that you have understood the text.
- Comparing texts means discussing the similarities and differences between them. You should focus on the purpose and audience of the texts, the content of the arguments and the quality (evaluation) of the arguments.

Activity 14

You are going to write the next paragraph in the comparison essay.

1 Discuss with a partner how Terence Blacker and Bruce Anderson use different examples of men crying to back up their arguments. List two or three points of similarity and/or difference.

2 On your own, write a paragraph comparing how the two texts use examples of men crying. Follow the guidelines on page 88.

Writing to inform, explain, describe

Writing to inform

> **My learning**
>
> In 'Writing to inform' I will:
> - review the key features of information texts
> - practise writing information texts that have clear language, format and structure
> - think about the importance of purpose and audience.

Information texts include encyclopedias, information leaflets and travel guides. All information texts tell the reader about someone or something, and this is what you should aim to do, as clearly as possible, when writing an information text.

> **Activity 15**
>
> 1 Read the following text, which comes at the beginning of a book for teachers.
>
> 2 The notes around the text describe some of the features of information texts like this. Read the notes, then answer the questions and give examples as instructed.

The opening sentence is a **general statement**. Why do you think the author puts this at the beginning?

The more detailed information is displayed as **bullet points**. What are the advantages of using this device?

The writer makes it **clear** what the subject of each sentence is. How does she do this?

Formal language. Find two more examples of formal language.

The **present tense** is used. Find three more examples.

The **third person** (she/he) is used. Why doesn't the author use 'I', 'you' or 'we'?

The writer uses **precise vocabulary**, including **technical terms** relating to subject matter. Find two other examples.

Boys and girls are different

Although the environment in which children are nurtured clearly affects the way they turn out, research into gender shows that there are significant physical and behavioural differences between boys and girls from birth.

- Baby girls in the first few hours of life are much more interested in people and faces, while baby boys are as happy if objects are dangled in front of them.
- On average girls say their first words and learn to speak in short sentences earlier than boys.
- Boys are more active than girls, moving faster and spending more time in motion; girls spend more time in communication.
- Girls read earlier than boys and find it easier to cope with grammar, spelling and punctuation.
- Boys have better 'spatial ability' which gives them superior hand–eye co-ordination for ball games, enables them to visualise easily in three dimensions, and makes them better than girls at construction, map-reading and chess.

Adapted from L. Neall, *Bringing out the Best in Boys*

Practise IT

Bullets
You may want to present some of your writing (or notes) in the assignment as bullet points or numbered points. The best way to do this is to list all the points as usual, each one on a new line. Then select the text. Click 'Format', then 'Bullets and numbering' on the main toolbar, or you can click on the icons of bullets or numbered lists on the formatting toolbar.

Activity 16

1 In small groups, discuss some of the similarities and differences in the leisure activities of teenage boys and girls.

2 On your own, choose three or four of the points made in the discussion. Turn them into information bullet points. Introduce them with a single sentence, as in the text on page 90. Try to make your information text as clear and straightforward as possible. Use some of the techniques that are highlighted in the annotations around the text.

Purpose and audience

The writer of any text, including information texts, must keep the audience and the purpose of the text in mind. The precise language and structure of an information text depends on its purpose and audience.

Activity 17

1 Read the newspaper report on page 92.

2 Working with a partner, compare the features of an information text with those in 'Boys and girls are different' (page 90). Talk about how the features suit the different audience and purpose of each text.

3 Draw up a table like the one below and complete it to organise your thoughts.

	1: 'Boys and girls are different'	2: 'Death of the ladette'	How this suits the purpose and audience
Formal language	Very formal, e.g. technical terms and complex words like 'visualise'.	Some informal words, e.g. 'ladette', 'telly'.	Purpose of Text 1 is more serious – advising teachers. Text 2 is a popular newspaper, with entertainment as one aim.
Tense used	Present throughout	Mix of present and past tense	
Sentence structure – length and type			
Organisation of ideas			
Visual presentation			
Use of quotations			

DEATH OF THE LADETTE

Old-fashioned girls don't want to party

■ by LAURA NEILL

BRITISH women are rejecting the ladette lifestyle for an old-fashioned family role.

They're turning their backs on the hard-partying image made famous by the likes of Sarah Cox, 31, and Zoe Ball, 34.

Instead the so-called "new traditionalists" are married with children.

And they put the family before money and career, though they can combine both.

The new generation of 25 to 45-year-olds have been identified in a new survey.

They admire the values of their mother's era and believe in cooking and knitting, which has become trendy with the stars.

Twist

They snub food fads but know enough about health issues to realise what they should and shouldn't eat, according to the study for drinks firm Ovaltine.

Interviews with 500 women in the 25-45 age group found many wanted life to be "more like the old days" with a modern twist.

They believe in cooking meals for the family and not relying on fast food and dinner from a packet.

Instead of going out on the town, the new traditionalist prefers a "girls' night in".

A group of friends will gather at the home of one of their gang for a gossip.

Seven out of 10 women also thought life was probably better 50 years ago.

The emergence of the new traditionalist marks a swing away from the "having it all" breed to one who puts the family first, said the study.

Its findings illustrate what hit telly show *Ladette to Lady* aimed to

■ OUT OF DATE: Sara Cox, above, and, left, Ladette to Lady girls

KNIT WANTED: Girls would rather knit than be a ladette like Zoe Ball, above

Photo © Southern News & Pictures

Daily Star, 10 September 2005
copyright © Express Newspapers Ltd

Speaking and listening

Speaking and listening Opportunity

AO1(i) *Communicate clearly and imaginatively, structuring and organising your talk and using Standard English appropriately*
This is an ***individual speaking*** activity. It will be used to assess how well you can ***explain/describe/narrate***.

On your own, use your table to plan a presentation comparing the two information texts. Remember to:

- structure your talk well: begin with an introduction and take each point in turn
- explain what the similarities and differences are, quoting from the texts to back up your points
- speak clearly and slowly, using Standard English.

To gain good marks you need to:
- *speak confidently and fluently*
- *adapt the style of your talk to the needs of your audience*
- *show that you really understand the subject matter*
- *speak in Standard English, using a range of vocabulary and grammatical structures*
- *respond to questions or comments in an appropriate way.*

Structure and planning

Before writing any text, you must plan it. A good plan will help you to organise your ideas. It will also ensure that your writing is well structured. How you plan an information text will depend on the precise nature of the text. Newspaper reports are often organised like this:

Assignment tip

Spider diagrams can be a useful tool in the assignment room; you can use them to brainstorm ideas for a piece of writing. You can also use them to plan information texts that don't have an emphasis on the logical order of information. Put the subject in the centre bubble, then surround it with the main topics that you want to cover – in any order, just as you think of them (you can leave some out later if you want to). Draw lines to connect the main topics to any further points, examples or details. In longer information texts, the main topic bubbles often sum up a single paragraph or section.

Main idea – summed up in headline and opening paragraphs

More details – including background, quotes, etc.

Extra information – perhaps further comments, or widening the focus of the story

Activity 18

1 Check if 'Death of the ladette' (page 92) follows this structure. If so, where are the three sections?

2 Write a note about why you think newspaper reports are organised like this.

3 'Boys and girls are different' (page 90) is a different kind of information text. What planning tool do you think the author used?

Activity 19

Imagine that two 'warrior women' have been found preserved in the ice in an Alpine pass, armed with bows and spears. Archaeologists have dated them to 50,000 BC. You have been asked to write a short report on the discovery for a popular newspaper.

1 Working with a partner, brainstorm ideas for the report; you could use a spider diagram. Invent some information about the discovery and some comments, e.g. from the leader of the expedition and from a professor of History at Geneva University.

2 Using three different colours, highlight your 'main idea', 'further details' and 'extra information'.

3 Turn your notes into a three-part diagram like the one on page 93.

Practise IT

Text colour
To highlight specific blocks of text you can change the colour and font style to make it stand out. First you will need to select the text you wish to highlight, then right-click on it, and then select Font from the list that appears. In the pop-up box you can then click on the font colour drop-down list and select the colour you want. The click on OK and your text will be changed. Make sure that the colour you choose does not make the text unreadable on the page!

Quoting the experts

Look at how the 'expert' comment is introduced by the writer of 'Death of the ladette' (see page 92).

> Lifestyle guru Rita Konig, author of *Domestic Bliss*, said: 'As our daily lives get more frenetic, there seems to be a stronger leaning towards the vintage styles and traditional values of past generations.'

Note how the speaker's name comes first, followed by what she says. This is a common convention in newspaper reports: it makes it quite clear who is being quoted. Note how 'Lifestyle guru Rita Konig' is more punchy and direct than 'Rita Konig, who is a lifestyle guru and author ...'. Note also how punctuation helps the reader. The extra information 'author of *Domestic Bliss*' is embedded in the sentence, marked off by two commas. The inverted commas show what is being said. Remember to use commas and inverted commas correctly in your own writing.

> ### Activity 20
>
> Think of something one of your experts could have said about the 'warrior women'. Write a sentence structured like the newspaper example above that makes it clear to the reader who the expert is and what their comment is.

Writing your report

> ### Activity 21
>
> 1 Draft your complete report on the 'warrior women'. Follow the plan that you outlined in Activity 20. The newspaper editor is allowing you space for only seven or eight sentences, so you have to be concise and punchy.
>
>   You may like to use some of these sentence starters:
>   *Two warrior women have been discovered …*
>   *Archaeologists have confirmed that …*
>   *Leader of the expedition Titus Gorman, 34, said …*
>   *Women's groups are excited by …*
>
> 2 Swap your draft with a partner's. Comment on how well the language and structure in your partner's draft suit the purpose and audience of the task.
>
> 3 Make revisions to your draft in the light of your partner's comments.

Assignment tip

The piece of writing that you will have to do for your assignment will not be wholly information based. You will be assessed in your skills in writing to 'inform, explain, describe'. Read the question carefully. There may be a section which is more information based, and one which is more explanation based, for example. Many of the writing skills practised here apply to different text types.

Key points

- When writing an information text, make sure that its language, format and structure are as clear as possible.
- You must also take purpose and audience into account. In a newspaper report, for example, it is often effective to start the article with some key points, then backtrack to give the context.

Writing to explain

> **My learning**
>
> In 'Writing to explain' I will:
> - review the key features of explanation texts
> - practise planning an explanation text that has a clear structure
> - practise using connectives and writing sentences of different types
> - write an explanation text of my own.

Explanation texts such as science textbooks or 'How to …' guides, tell the reader how or why something happens – how something works, how you do something, or what causes something. Explanation texts often contain a lot of information, but it is the *how* or *why* rather than the *what* that is important.

Activity 22

The text below and the one on page 97 come from a book that sets out to explain how and why men and women are different. The annotations around the first text illustrate some features of language and structure that are often found in explanation texts.

Your task is to find similar features in the second text. Draw up and complete a table like the one below, listing examples of the features that show this is an explanation text. In the third column, comment on how effective you think each feature is.

Example	Feature	Comment
'Women hear better than men ...'	Clear statement of what is being explained.	Makes it clear from the start what the passage is about.

Begins with a general statement to introduce the topic.

Short, well-structured sentences for clarity.

Topic sentences at start of paragraph to state main point.

Past tense to explain what happened in the past. Present tense to explain what happens in the present.

Structure: a series of logical steps. New paragraph for each step in the explanation.

Humorous title makes explanation more accessible.

Language that shows how things are connected (casual language)

Subject of sentence at start, to make it clear what sentence is about.

Later sentences in paragraph develop the main point with examples.

Technical and precise vocabulary.

Formal language throughout.

Different job specs

Men and women have evolved differently because they had to. Men hunted, women gathered. Men protected, women nurtured. As a result, their bodies and brains evolved in completely different ways.

As their bodies physically changed to adapt to their specific functions, so did their minds. Men grew taller and stronger than most women, while their brains developed to suit their tasks. Women were mostly content for men to work away as they kept the cave fires burning, and their brains evolved to cope with their function in life.

Over millions of years, the brain structures of men and women thus continued to change in different ways. Now, we know the sexes process information differently. They think differently. They believe different things. They have different perceptions, priorities and behaviours.

To pretend otherwise is a recipe for heartache, confusion, and disillusionment all your life.

Allan and Barbara Pease, *Why Men Don't Listen and Women Can't Read Maps*

Women hear better than men and are excellent at distinguishing high-pitched sounds. A woman's brain is programmed to hear a baby cry in the night, whereas a father may be oblivious to it and sleep on. If there is a
5 kitten crying in the distance, a woman will hear it. A man, however, with his superior spatial and directional skills, can tell her where it is.

At one week, a baby girl can distinguish her mother's voice or the cry of another baby from the other sounds that are
10 present in the same room. A baby boy can't. Males use their left brain only for listening but females use both brains for this task. The female brain has the ability to separate and categorise sound and make decisions about each sound. This accounts for a woman's ability to listen to one person
15 in a face-to-face conversation while monitoring another person's conversation. It also explains why a man has difficulty hearing a conversation while there is a television on in the background or dishes are being clattered in the sink. If a phone rings, a man will demand people stop
20 talking, music is turned down and the TV is switched off for him to answer it. A woman simply answers the phone.

Allan and Barbara Pease, *Why Men Don't Listen and Women Can't Read Maps*

Structure and planning

If you are going to write a clear explanation, you must pay attention to the structure of your text. That means planning before you write. One planning tool that suits explanation texts well is an adapted version of a spider diagram.

Each bubble represents one stage in the explanation. The label in the bubble is the main point (often the topic sentence of the paragraph). The lines branching off each bubble develop the main point, by giving examples or going into more detail.

Activity 23

The plan started below shows how 'Different job specs' (page 96) is structured. Discuss with a partner how you would complete it to summarise the structure of the rest of the text.

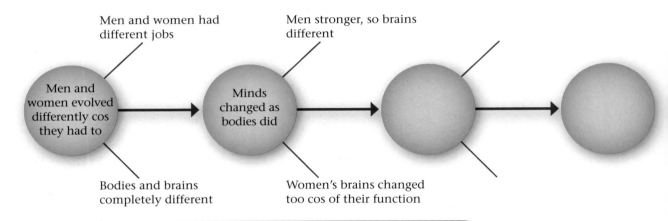

Activity 24

You are a member of your school council. You are suggesting that from now on, boys and girls will have PE lessons separately. Your task is to write a letter to parents, outlining your suggestion and explaining the reasons for it.

1 Brainstorm some ideas with a partner. For example:
   • different sexes like different sports
   • less chance of distraction
   • embarrassment factor
   • possibility of injury in contact sports.

2 On your own, plan the structure of your letter. Choose the most important points and create a diagram like the one above. Add notes where you think you can develop each point by giving further detail or examples. You could begin like this:

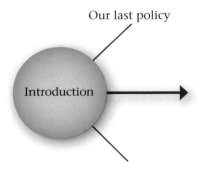

Assignment tip

Assignment tip

Don't waste time in the assessment room trying to construct complex diagrams on the computer. A pen and paper sketch is much faster and more efficient. It's more important to focus on what you are saying and how your thoughts are connected than to play with the drawing function on your word-processing program.

Using connectives

When you are explaining something, you need to signpost to the reader where your sentences – your thoughts – are going. Look back at the text on men and women's hearing, on page 97. Notice how each of the following connectives has a precise purpose.

1 '*whereas* a father' (lines 3–4). This word contrasts the new subject (father) with the previous one (mother).
2 '*If* there is a kitten' (lines 4–5). 'If' highlights the fact that this is a cause, which will be followed by an effect ('a woman will hear it').
3 'A man, *however*' (lines 5–6). The word 'however' shows that the writer is contrasting the man's behaviour with the woman's.
4 '*but* females' (line 11). 'but' shows that something different or contrasting is going to be said here.
5 '*This accounts for*' (line 14). This is another way of saying: 'All this is an explanation for the following.'
6 '*It also explains*' (line 16). This shows that another explanation is coming.

Signposts like these allow the reader to keep on track of the explanation. Other signposts that are particularly useful in explanation (causal) writing are: *because, as a result, therefore, for example, the reason why, so.*

Activity 25

Write one explanation from your planned Activity 24 letter in full. Do this in just two or three sentences. Make sure you signpost your explanation clearly by using connectives.

Using different sentence structures

The writers of the texts on men and women on pages 96 and 97 have used sentences of different lengths and different types. This is for two reasons:
• for variety and interest
• to do different jobs.

Activity 26

Look at the explanations below of different sentence constructions along with some examples from the text on page 97.

> Simple sentences have only one clause. They are useful when you need to make a straightforward point in a simple way. They can also work well after a series of long sentences, for variety or shock value.
>
> Example: *A woman simply answers the phone.*

1 Find this simple sentence in the text. Think about what makes it effective.

2 Write a simple sentence of your own, which you will include in your school council letter.

> Compound sentences are two or more simple sentences linked by *and*, *but* or *or*. They are useful when you need to add another point in a straightforward way. However, *and* doesn't always show exactly how your ideas are related, and using it too many times can make a passage dull.
>
> Example: *Males use their left brain only for listening but females use both brains for this task.*

3 Find this compound sentence in the text. Think about what makes it effective.

4 Write a compound sentence of your own, which you will include in your school council letter.

> Complex sentences have one main clause and at least one subordinate clause. They are useful when you need to make precise links between ideas. They are often longer sentences, which can make them more interesting to read.
>
> Example: *If a phone rings, a man will demand people stop talking, music is turned down and the TV is switched off for him to answer it.*

5 Find this complex sentence in the text. Work out how each clause is related to its neighbour (hint: each clause has its own verb).

6 Find two other complex sentences in the texts. Be prepared to explain what makes them effective.

7 Write a complex sentence of your own, which you will include in your school council letter.

Assignment tip

Sometimes when planning or drafting your writing task in the exam, you will think of a way to improve your reading task answer, especially if it is on the same triplet (e.g. inform, explain, describe). Make a note of this, then when you have time, open up the other file and make the change.

Assignment tip

The assignment may ask you to write from the point of view of someone else, e.g. a headteacher. It's important to stick to the same 'voice' throughout. That means:

- maintaining the point of view, e.g. not suddenly becoming a student, or a parent, or yourself
- maintaining the tone, e.g. not suddenly becoming humorous when the topic is a serious one
- maintaining the formality, e.g. not including slang words in a formal text.

When you read through your writing, check that your voice has remained consistent throughout.

Key points

- The main purpose of an explanation text is to lead someone through a process. When writing an explanation text, make sure its language and structure are as clear as possible.
- Think about the purpose and audience of an explanation text before you write it.
- Use connectives to make the links between your ideas clear.
- Use sentences of different lengths for variety and effect. Complex sentences are good for showing the links between your ideas.

Activity 27

Now draft your letter, following the plan that you drew up in Activity 24.

1 Think about the purpose and audience of your letter, and the effect these will have on its style. How clear does it need to be? How formal will the language be? Is humour appropriate?

2 Swap your draft with a partner's and read each other's work carefully. Decide what works well and highlight this on the draft. Discuss how to improve your partner's explanation text – write up to three suggestions on their draft.

3 Redraft the selected sections of your own text, using your partner's comments to guide you.

Writing to describe

My learning

In 'Writing to describe' I will:
- *review the key features of descriptive texts*
- *explore in more detail techniques of good descriptive language*
- *think about good paragraphing, grabbing the readers' attention and effective punctuation*
- *try writing my own descriptive passage.*

Most writing tasks can be improved by good descriptive writing – whether you are writing narrative, a letter home or telling your life story. If you can describe something or someone imaginatively and effectively, then you will engage the interest of your audience.

Describing an incident

Activity 28

In the text opposite, the author is describing an incident to show what life is like in an all-male household. The annotations in yellow illustrate some of the features of descriptive text. The questions in green ask you to think about the author's techniques.

Read the text, discuss the annotations with a partner, and answer the questions in note form. Be prepared to feed back your responses to the class.

A picture of the scene is drawn straight away: no introduction.

Similes to emphasise and depict the quality of the voice.

Simple but powerful metaphor to show its effect.

Powerful verb.

Present tense throughout makes scene immediate to the reader.

Humorous comment shows author's attitude to the woman.

Use of semi-colon to vary sentence structure.

Short sentence to end paragraph, for effect.

I'm driving Alexander down a dusty beach road to the pie cart. A woman waiting on the bank takes one look at us and loses control – so much so I assume she's on drugs (or perhaps she's *not* on drugs – keeping up your medication isn't as easy as it sounds). 'What the *hell* do you think you're doing!' she cries. She's doing the voice that only angry mothers can do, it sounds like a power saw biting into timber. No, it sounds like one of those kung-fu fighting cries; it's like someone throwing a javelin into your ear. It's a voice that frightens Alexander far more than anything we've been doing driving round the park; and actually, because this voice goes to the roots of men, it rather frightens me too. Suddenly, both of us are five years old.

'*Get* that child off your windscreen,' she shrieks, 'you *bloody* fool!' We're driving at ten kilometres an hour and Alexander is sitting on the windscreen; she assumes he's in danger. But what danger she sees that I don't is unclear.

Why does the author ask a question here? How else could he have made the point?

What is the author implying about the husband here? Why doesn't he say it directly?

Which words in this paragraph are powerful? Explain why they are effective.

How does the author manage to both laugh at himself and make a serious point in the final paragraph? Does it work?

What effect does 'add his voice to hers' have?

Why is direct speech used here? Why the italics?

Why does the author use these two examples here?

How does the time perspective shift in the final paragraph? How does the tense of the verbs show this?

He's holding on to one of the windscreen wipers, he's got both feet firmly on the middle of the bonnet, what's the problem? And it seemed it wasn't just a woman thing because her husband comes up to the car to add his voice to hers. 'You're *crazy*,' he says. 'You irresponsible *fool*!'

I suppose in marriage you have to support your spouse. 'Back me up!' we say, whenever we say or do something indefensible, like making children turn off *The Simpsons* because it's dinner time, or shrieking at amiable strangers peacefully driving their sons on the bonnet of their car.

Two years later I had devised the perfect retort to them both. I should have drawn myself up to my full height, as you are supposed to do in these situations, and said: 'Bite me.' That would have taught Alexander how to stick up for himself without being offensive. That's one of the most important lessons in life.

Simon Carr, *The Boys are Back in Town*

Good paragraphing

The paragraph is a key tool in structuring any piece of writing. Just as a sentence is one complete idea that makes sense on its own, so paragraphs are collections of sentences that form a single 'block' of sense. When you want to move on to a new point, or a new character, or a new place or time, then you probably need to start a new paragraph.

- Long paragraphs allow you to develop an idea or a scene in depth, but they can lose the attention of the reader.
- Short paragraphs are easier to read (especially in newspapers, where columns are so narrow) but can be unsatisfying after a while.
- Varying the length of your paragraphs keeps the reader's interest, just as varying sentence length does.

Activity 29

1 Re-read the text on page 103.

2 In pairs, discuss why the author starts his paragraphs where he does.

3 Could this author have used paragraphs differently, and what effect would that have had?

Be prepared to feed back your ideas to the class.

Grabbing attention from the start

A passage of descriptive writing can be effective at the start of a text with a more serious aim – for example a newspaper report or piece of explanation. It grabs the readers' attention and makes them want to read on.

Activity 30

Read the start of the newspaper report opposite. Then discuss these following questions with a partner, and make some notes.

1 How does the first paragraph differ in style from the second?

2 Why are they different? Think about the purpose of each paragraph.

3 What makes the first paragraph a good piece of descriptive writing? Think about:
- the detail
- the individual words
- the shape of the sentences.

Practise IT

Paragraphing
When keying in your writing, make sure your method of paragraphing is clear and consistent. There are two main ways of creating a new paragraph.

1 **To create indented paragraphs:** hit the enter/return key once: to start a new line, then the tab key once to indent.

2 **To create line-spaced paragraphs:** hit the enter/return key twice. (Hitting it only once will start a new line, but will not give you a clear space between the paragraphs.)

Cut and paste into a new document a page-sized piece of prose from the Internet, or from another Word file. Turn each sentence into a new paragraph, first using Method 1, then Method 2. Which is easier and/or quicker for you? Choose the method you prefer and stick to it.

Games for girls

Jessica Kiddle

HER manicured fingers are damaged from perpetual button-bashing. The children's dinner is burning in the oven. But all will be well so long as she can take out this last wave of Sith Assassins and restore the planet Dantooine to the hands of the Republic.

That scenario is not real but, judging by the number of suburban housewives playing on X-Boxes and PlayStations, it could be. Female players are now opening up the world of computer games – previously the domain of teenage boys. In 2003, a survey published in America by the Entertainment Software Association showed that more women over the age of 18 'game' than teenage boys …

The Scotsman, *9 March 2005*

Activity 31

Imagine you are writing a newspaper story describing how dancing classes for boys are proving more popular than boxing in your local youth club. You want to begin by grabbing the reader's attention with a piece of descriptive writing. Draft the first paragraph of your story.

1 Focus on one individual.

2 Think carefully about your language, sentence structure and punctuation.
   You could begin like this:
   > *Brent Cooper stroked his chin and flexed his muscles. This was going to be difficult. Then he stepped into the ring and …*

3 Finally, write the first sentence of the second paragraph, which gives the background to the story. Use a plainer and more informative style, as in the newspaper article above.

Practising descriptive language

Here are four good techniques to help you make your writing really descriptive.

- Go into **detail**. This roots the description in something specific. It helps the reader to picture the scene exactly.
- Use **powerful words**. Choose your words carefully, especially adjectives and verbs, which will add colour and impact to your description.
- Include some **imagery**. Similes, metaphors and personification paint a picture in the reader's mind.
- Appeal to the **senses**. What are people feeling, seeing, hearing, smelling, tasting?

Activity 32

In 2004 Ellen MacArthur set out to become the fastest person to sail round the world on her own.

Read the email below, which she sent on Day 21 of her voyage. In pairs discuss the questions in the boxes.

Delete   Reply   Reply All   Forward   Print

Last night was a dark night, hard to see anything out there – nothing but the constant noise of B&Q[1] speeding through the water, the howling wind and the breaking of the waves. The waves are so steep here that poor B&Q feels like she's either running down a hill or being pushed hard up one. Waves regularly break on the windward float quarter. What is noticeable through the dark, shining brighter than our glowing instruments, are the crests of phosphorescence[2] – unbelievable, beautiful, and at times immense. We spend our time, even when trying to rest huddled in a ball in the cuddy,[3] just feeling where we are on each mountain, how fast, how far and when will we hit the bottom …

Last night I did a series of sail changes which had the adrenalin pumping hard – wind speeds were up above 45 knots, and our surfs were regularly over 30 knots. (And all this while plummeting down unpredictable slopes of black powerful sea in the dark …)

Sunrise, though, was amazing – the light fantastic, and the seabirds, as ever, around us all the time. Wandering albertrosses, black-bellied storm petrels, and little sheerwaters – dancing not just in the wind but with the immense waves. I guess for them it's just another day in the Southern Ocean.

Ellen MacArthur, *Race against Time*

Where does Ellen use her **senses** in this passage?

Where does she use the **imagery** of waves as mountains? How does she develop this?

Ellen refers to **details** of the boat and its speed. What is the effect of this?

Identify three **powerful words** in the second paragraph. Explain your choice.

[1] Ellen's boat.
[2] Tiny sea creatures that glow in the dark.
[3] Small sheltered area on board.

Activity 33

Imagine you are Ellen MacArthur entering Falmouth harbour on 7 February 2005, having beaten the world record. Write your final email describing the scene. Your aim is to entertain the reader with the quality of your description.

1 Imagine the scene – home after 71 gruelling days at sea, hundreds of boats surrounding *B&Q*, crowds lining the harbour. Jot down some things that you are seeing, hearing and feeling.

2 Draft your email. Use the present tense to make it vivid and immediate: 'I am …'

Using punctuation correctly and effectively

Punctuation has several functions.
- It can make the meaning clear.
- It can make it easier for readers, for example, by telling them where to pause for breath.
- It can help you to extend sentences to make them more varied and effective.

So it's worth paying attention to punctuation when you write.

Activity 34

Read this short extract from the text on page 103.
Pay attention to the punctuation.

> 'What the *hell* do you think you're doing!' she cries. She's doing the voice that only angry mothers can do, it sounds like a power saw biting into timber. No, it sounds like one of those kung-fu fighting cries; it's like someone throwing a javelin into your ear.

Now answer these questions.

1 What punctuation is used to show that speech is being quoted directly?

2 What does the apostrophe in *you're* tell you about what *you're* means? Find one other word in the passage that uses an apostrophe in the same way.

3 An exclamation mark never has a full stop after it, even if it is at the end of a sentence or ends a passage of direct speech. Does the same apply to a question mark?

4 Why does the author put a comma after *No*?

5 Why has the author used a semi-colon in the last sentence? How else could he have punctuated this sentence?

6 The apostrophe in *it's* shows that it stands for 'it is'. Write another sentence using 'its' without an apostrophe, to show that you know the difference in meaning.

Assignment tip

Only the final draft of your responses to the tasks must be word-processed and saved at the end of the assignment. If you want to, you can write all your first drafts by hand; but you will need to leave a large amount of time at the end to key in your final drafts, and you will have to type quickly and accurately. If you don't finish in time, your handwritten notes will not be accepted.

Key points

- If you can describe something or someone imaginatively and effectively, then you will engage the interest of your audience.
- Four techniques used in good descriptive writing are: going into detail, using powerful words, including imagery, and appealing to the senses.
- Start a new paragraph when you want to move on to a new point, or a new character, or a new place or time.
- Correct punctuation adds meaning and impact to your writing.

Checking and redrafting

Good writers will check their material and redraft it if necessary. You will always find things that you can correct or improve, such as typos, misspellings, and words and sentences that could be better expressed.

Activity 35

1 Read your draft description from Activity 33 again.
  - Can you make any of your adjectives or verbs more powerful?
  - Can you include some imagery, or develop an image that you have used?
  - Have you used punctuation clearly and effecti vely

2 Redraft the selected sections of your text, so that you have a version you are happy with.

F Assignment practice: Reading non-fiction texts and writing to inform, explain, describe

In your assignment for Unit 1B you will have one complete assignment covering:
• Reading media texts
• Writing to argue, persuade, advise
• Reading non-fiction texts
• Writing to inform, explain, describe

You will already have studied the media and non-fiction texts which will be on the same theme. You will have a total of four hours in which to do the complete assignment. The four tasks in Unit 1B are together worth 30% of your final mark for Single Award GCSE English or English Studies.

The following assignment gives you the opportunity to practice the skills you have been learning for reading non-fiction texts and writing to inform, explain, describe. There is also detailed guidance on how to tackle this practice assignment on pages 115–117.

On pages 54–57 you will find the practice assignment for the first part:
• Reading media texts
• Writing to argue, persuade, advise

In your **Reading** responses you need to show that:
• you understand the texts, and what they are arguing
• you can describe how language and structure contribute to the argument
• you can say how effective the arguments are
• you can select the right information to answer the questions.

In your **Writing** responses you need to show:
• that you can communicate your ideas clearly and imaginatively
• that you can write for a particular purpose and audience
• that you can organise your ideas in sentences and paragraphs
• that you can use words and sentence structures effectively
• that your spelling and punctuation are accurate.

TOGETHER OR APART?

You have a maximum of 4 hours to complete all the tasks below and on page 54.

You must study the following non-fiction texts (pages 116–9) in order to complete this task.
- 'The benefits of co-education'
- 'Girls and boys together'
- 'Are girls short-changed in the co-ed classroom?'
- 'What's good about single-sex schools?'

Stage 2: Analysing the arguments

You are a member of the school council. You have been asked to consider whether there should be more single-sex schools, as many people demand. You have been given some non-fiction texts to look at.

Task 3

Your task is to use the non-fiction texts in order to write an e-mail that outlines each side of the debate for the other school council members. In your e-mail you should:
- identify a number of arguments that put forward the two sides of the debate in the non-fiction texts
- show clearly how these non-fiction texts present their view of single sex schools.

You should write in continuous prose.

In this task you will be assessed for your reading skills.

(20 marks for Reading)

Stage 3: Reporting back

Task 4

You have now made your decision about the future of schools in your area. You have to write a report to the education committee, informing them of your decision, and explaining your reasons. You must describe one or two examples of excellent schools to back up your decision. These descriptions can be in the form of eyewitness reports.

You can decide either to make more schools single-sex, or to reduce the number of single-sex schools.

You will be assessed for your skills in writing to inform, explain, describe.

(20 marks for Writing)

Text 1

An extract from the prospectus of Loretto School, by Michael Mavor, the Headmaster

---

The benefits of co-education

I'm not in any way against single-sex schools – it's more important that a school should be good. I favour co-education for the following reasons.

At some point in their lives boys and girls need to learn to work together. It's good preparation for the real world, and I don't agree that pupils at co-ed schools cannot attain the same academic standards.

From my own experience as an English teacher, you can teach English in a much more interesting way to a mixed class. You get more points of view, which make discussions all the more lively.

Girls in the Sixth Form at Loretto have been doing very well across the sciences, and particularly in physics. Many of them go on to study medicine.

Being co-ed provides Loretto with a ready-made community, which has considerable advantages in terms of activities like drama and music.

Many Lorettonians do the Gold Duke of Edinburgh Award. This gives boys and girls an opportunity to see how the others work under stress. Again, it's useful experience for the real world.

We held a charity concert for Tsunami Relief as well as a charity fashion show. These events show that boys and girls lead in different ways. It's perhaps a bit of a cliché, but boys tend to be more traditional in their approach and girls more radical. Clearly it's healthy for our senior pupils to learn the proper mix of these two approaches.

We have a seven-day week here, and boys and girls have busy lives with academic studies and all the activities. They also have social lives, and these have to be fitted in along with everything else. This teaches what I describe as the 'right sort of toughness'. Life at a co-ed school is more complex than a single-sex school but, I believe, more fun.

Families tend to be very busy, particularly if both parents work – many of our parents appreciate being able to send their sons and daughters to the same school. Logistically it has many advantages, but other benefits are the stability and sense of community that it gives, particularly for bigger families.

However, I'm all for choice and parents should be able to choose whether to send their children to a co-ed school or a single-sex school.

Text 2

An extract from a newspaper analysis of the merits of single-sex or co-educational schools

Girls and boys together

Proponents of co-education point to powerful pressures that encourage educating girls and boys under the same roof. Simple logistics in a busy world make schooling sons and daughters together attractive.

'Co-ed schools accord with parents' demands – it's easier to have all the family's children at school in one place,' said Jean Hall, founder of a management consultancy that has helped a number of schools embrace the change. 'Working mums and dads don't have time to liaise with different schools.'

Mixed schools are also the norm in the British state sector: the single-sex institutions largely disappeared in the 1960s and 1970s when they were merged to form comprehensives. Out of 3000 state secondary schools, just 184 cater only for boys and 226 for girls.

Like others, Hall also argues that co-education is the best preparation for a 'co-educational' world. 'It provides preparation for life after school, including the workplace,' she said.

Some parents believe it helps girls and boys learn to understand each other early on, rather than being suddenly flung together at university.

David Pierce, 19, and now at Hull University, attended first a boys' school then a co-ed. 'At a single-sex school you don't get to hear about girls' problems: you have less knowledge about them,' he said. 'You wouldn't be able to talk to girls on a friendly basis, you wouldn't have as much experience of talking to girls.'

Katie Banks, 23, and now working at a media firm in London as an intern, went to a girls-only school and said: 'There was a lack of banter in the classroom – boys bring a different perspective. And then you suddenly get launched into university and it's a bit like a sweetshop. You weren't used to seeing boys as friends – they were potential boyfriends.'

Despite those drawbacks, however, Pierce found that single-sex schools had one distinct advantage. He preferred it for sport because in a co-ed school 'girls could always run faster than me, which was a major embarrassment'.

Text 3

A statement by the Girls' Schools Association

"

Are girls short-changed in the co-ed classroom?

Research in both the UK and USA over the last 20 years has indicated that for many girls, a co-ed classroom does not help them to achieve equality, but indeed may depress self-confidence and limit aspirations. Many girls are short-changed by the co-ed classroom.

- **Boys dominate teacher time.** Classroom observations showed that boys answer and ask more questions, hog the teacher's attention and the apparatus, organise themselves more quickly and ruthlessly to their tasks, while girls hang back through shyness or a desire to be helpful and co-operative. Boys are more demanding of teachers' time both behaviourally and academically.

- **Girls are less likely to take intellectual risks and are more passive.** They fear getting it wrong, looking silly, being considered stupid, being judged by their male peers and found wanting. They prefer to solve problems by team working.

- **Subject choices are more likely to be polarised.** In co-ed schools both boys and girls are more likely to choose traditional male and female subjects. This limits choice and aspirations for both boys and girls.

- **Girls tend to lose self-esteem and confidence** as they progress through adolescence. This is made worse if they are constantly being placed under social pressure from boys. A co-ed environment does not always give them the space and security in which to build up their self-esteem and confidence in their own abilities as individuals.

- **Less positive role models for girls.** Co-ed schools do not always provide girls with the necessary positive role models through the teaching staff and the general ethos and philosophy of the school that is so essential for building girls' self-esteem and confidence. This is particularly the case for schools that have gone co-ed but where girls are in a minority. These are essentially still boys' schools with all the male traditions and trappings.

- **Girls mature physically, mentally and emotionally earlier than boys.** Girls and boys mature physically, mentally and emotionally at different ages. In a co-ed environment this is much more difficult to manage. Girls are likely to lose out, as they tend to mature earlier and may well be held back by slower developing boys.

- **Girls can have fewer opportunities for leadership roles** in co-ed schools.

"

Text 4

This is an extract from the 'Young People's Voices' section of a magazine called 0–19

WHAT'S GOOD ABOUT SINGLE-SEX SCHOOLS?

Martin Hemming talks to teenagers about single sex education.

Are they missing out or having a ball?

Choosing between a single-sex or mixed school can create a dilemma for children and parents. Parents often feel their children will be able to work harder at a single-sex school with fewer distractions; but what do young people themselves say about single-sex schools? Are girls more confident of their abilities without boys around? Do boys concentrate more without girls to distract them?

Fleur

My primary school, like most, was mixed, so I thought that with all girls it would be a bit weird.

But now I prefer going to an all-girls school. With boys around I wouldn't be able to work as hard. My dad prefers it that there are no boys.

There's no one to impress at a girls' school. People come in and say: 'Oh, I just got out of bed.' But that's all right because there's nobody to look good for. You can look bad at school and when you go out you can show everyone how good you can look.

If we did have a mixed school, I think by Year 11 you'd be bored of the boys anyway. You'd have already been out with every single one of them!

Jasmin

When I'm older, it's all going to depend on my education, so I'm just looking towards that really. I know I'll meet boys through the other stuff, like my youth club and the pantomime I'm in. You might not meet boys in secondary school, but you'll make friends with them at university or at work, so I wouldn't be too worried about it at the moment.

We have discos with boys' schools, but not many. But it's better like that. It makes you want to go to them more.

Gordon

At an all-boys' school there are fewer distractions, I'd say. With girls around I think we'd be more mouthy to the teachers, trying to show off. At a boys' school you can act yourself. When you're in Year 7 you're just happy being with your mates. But when you start seeing your mates talking to girls you think, 'I've got to try that.' You just get interested and then addicted!

Yajnah

Being in an all-girls' school you can be with your friends more. Boys distract you. At a girls school you can be closer to your friends, without being interrupted by boys. Although, just being girls, there are lots of arguments.

We have discos with the local boys' schools. I've been to some of them but I can't be bothered with them any more. Meeting boys isn't really the most important thing right now.

0–19 magazine, March 2005
email: zero2nineteen.magazine@rbi.co.uk

Assignment advice

Before you start

You have been given four non-fiction texts. In the actual assignment you will have studied these in class before seeing the assessment tasks. Here, you haven't had that luxury! Instead, this assignment gives you the opportunity to practise some basic reading skills – skimming and summarising.

In your actual GCSE assessment you can make notes during the assessment. You are not allowed, however, to take these notes out of the assessment room. You are also not allowed to take notes or annotated versions of the texts into the assessment room.

Scan each of the four texts in turn, and jot down the following.
- **Purpose** – what is the main point of view of the author?
- **Audience** – who is the writer addressing?
- **Key points** – note one or two of the main points that the writer is making
- **Impression** – note down your overall impression of the text. Is it difficult to follow? Is it satisfying to read? Does it stand out from the others in any way?

Stage 2: Analysing the argument

Task 3
You have been asked to identify and analyse a number of arguments outlining each side of the debate. Your first task, therefore, is to identify the arguments on both sides of the debate. Look back over the notes you have already made ('Before you start', above) and choose at least one text from each side of the debate. When making your choice, make sure you:
- understand what the writer is saying
- have something to say about it (you don't have to agree with it).

The task has been broken up into two sections.
- Identify a number of arguments that put forward the two sides of the debate in the non-fiction texts.
- Show clearly how these non-fiction texts present their view of single-sex schools.

Here is one possible plan.

> **Plan**
> - Begin with a short introduction, saying what you are going to do and why.
> - Summarise and evaluate the first argument you have chosen.
> - Summarise and evaluate the second argument on the opposing side.
> - Summarise and evaluate any further arguments you may be including.
> - End with a conclusion

Discuss with a partner the advantages and disadvantages of this method. Then decide if you are going to follow this plan or one of your own.

Note that in Stage 1 you are being assessed for your reading skills. You have already been 'put in role' as a member of the school council and you have to show that you understand the texts and can say interesting and useful things about them. You do have to write in continuous prose, however – notes are not acceptable.

Stage 3: Reporting back

Task 4
Here you are being assessed on the quality of your writing. You have been given a single writing task. Before you start planning, you need to 'get into role'. Think about:
- who you are supposed to be
- why you are writing (purpose)
- who you are writing for (audience)
- how this will affect the content and style of your writing.

In particular, you should think about these questions.
- How formal will your writing be? How reasonable, or emotional, will it be?
- Have you decided to make more schools single-sex, or reduce the number of single-sex schools?

Remember that you are being assessed for your skills in writing for three particular purposes: to **inform**, **explain**, **describe**.

The report is described as 'informing the teachers of your decision'. Jot down three or four key features of information writing to remind you to write to this purpose.

One important section of the report is explaining the two options available. Jot down three or four key features of explanation writing to remind you to write to this purpose.

You must include 'one or two descriptions' of schools that back up your decision. How can you make these eyewitness reports effective?

Here is a possible plan for your writing.
1 Introduction outlining the debate about single-sex education, and what the options are.
2 Section informing the committee of the decision you are making, and explaining why you have chosen this decision.
3 Section describing one or two schools to back up your decision.
4 Conclusion.

Now write your report. Remember to:
- use paragraphs
- check your writing carefully at the end (is it effective?; have you stayed 'in role'?)
- check the spelling, grammar and punctuation.

If you are keying in your final draft, check it one more time. Typing mistakes and other errors creep in when you type. Do not rely on a spellchecking device.

Checklist of learning

Reading non-fiction texts

1 Reading an argument
- An argument is a structured way of putting forward a point of view. Its purpose is to persuade the reader to agree with that point of view.
- Identifying the point of view is the first important step in understanding an argument.
- Summarise the key points of the argument in your own words; use the way the text is divided into paragraphs to help you.
- Arguments take account of their audience, just like other types of text.

2 Analysing an argument
- Analysing an argument means identifying the techniques used to back up a point of view.
- Points of view can be backed up by examples, opinions, facts, logic and counter-arguments.

3 The language of arguments
- Language can be used to back up the force of an argument.
- Effective arguments often include rhetorical techniques: Personal pronouns, Rhetorical questions, Effective words, Sound effects and Sentence skills (PRESS).
- You have to judge whether language effects, especially emotive language, unfairly bias the reader in favour of the argument.

4 Tricks and flaws in arguments
- Look out for any tricks or flaws in arguments that you read or hear.
- Common tricks and flaws are: anecdotal evidence, opinions presented as facts, exaggeration, abusing the opposition, over-generalising, selecting the evidence, irrelevance and inconsistency.

5 Evaluating arguments
- Evaluating an argument means using your knowledge of all the techniques used by the writer, plus your own challenges and thoughts about the argument, to assess how effective it is overall.
- Practise questioning and challenging any argument that you read or hear.

6 Quoting and comparing

- Only quote in full when the actual words of the original are important to the point you are making. Using your own words shows that you have understood what the text means.
- Comparing texts means discussing the similarities and differences between them. You should focus on the purpose and audience of the texts, the content of the arguments and the quality (evaluation) of the arguments.

Writing to inform, explain, describe

1 Writing to inform

- When writing an information text, make sure its language, format and structure are as clear as possible.
- You must also take its purpose and audience into account. In a newspaper report, for example, it is often effective to start the article with some key points, then backtrack to give the context.

2 Writing to explain

- The main purpose of an explanation text is to lead someone through a process. When writing an explanation text, make sure its language and structure are as clear as possible.
- Think about the purpose and audience of an explanation text before you write it.
- Use connectives to make the links between your ideas clear.
- Use sentences of different lengths for variety and effect. Complex sentences are good for showing the links between your ideas.

3 Writing to describe

- If you can describe something or someone imaginatively and effectively, then you will engage the interest of your audience.
- Four techniques used in good descriptive writing are: going into detail, using powerful words, including imagery and appealing to the senses.
- Start a new paragraph when you want to move on to a new point, or a new character, or a new place or time.
- Correct punctuation adds meaning and impact to your writing.

The following extracts show the different ways in which writing is used in six types of communication. The yellow boxes highlight the areas that are important to that communication type. They are followed by 'toolkits' which summarise the key points of each communication type (pages 125–6).

Formal letter

64 Queenscourt Drive
Highton
GR4 3PX
Tel. 01698 655433

The Manager
Highton Garage
Redhill Road
Highton
GR1 0NF

19 June 2006

Dear Sir or Madam

I am writing to enquire whether you have any vacancies, either now or in the near future, for an apprentice motor vehicle mechanic.

I have just completed my GNVQ course in Engineering at Highton FE College, and I would like to train as a motor mechanic. During Year 10 at school I did two weeks' work experience at Krazy Kars garage. I really enjoyed the work, and they gave me an excellent report.

I enclose a CV and a stamped addressed envelope for your reply. I look forward to hearing from you.

Yours faithfully

Liz Merchant

LIZ MERCHANT

Writer's address (no name) at top right of letter. Rest of letter is **'ranged left'**.

Recipient's name/title and address beneath, on left.

Date in full.

Greeting – 'Sir or Madam' used if name isn't known.

The **subject** of the letter is made clear in first paragraph . A **new paragraph** used for each new point.

Polite, **formal language** used.

Style is clear, factual and to the point. Letters for other purposes may have a different style to suit.

Formal ending: 'Yours faithfully' used if name of recipient isn't known. Otherwise 'Yours sincerely' is used.

Name printed (in capitals) after handwritten **signature**.

Webpage

title of website, with company logo and slogan

title of this webpage 'About Divine'. It is 'white out' on an orange band, to highlight its importance

underlined text shows a hyperlink – clicking on this takes the reader to another web page with more information

Related links: navigation bar to other websites that may be of interest

main navigation bar to link reader with main sections of the website. Note the first link ('Home'), which is to the website's home page (introductory page)

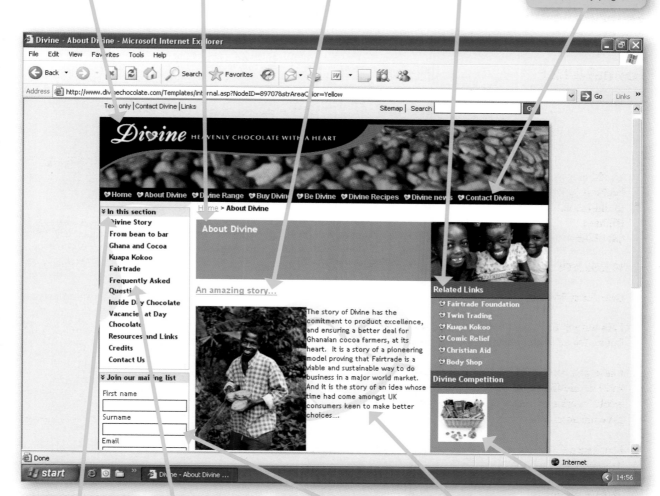

navigation bar to the other parts of the 'About Divine' section

Frequently Asked Questions: a common format for answering common readers' queries

marketing device to allow company to contact reader – showing the interactive power of websites

shirt burst of text, as the readers of web pages have short attention spans. The intention is to tempt reader in to follow the 'amazing story' further.

many photos to give web page visual appeal

design is an importent feature of web pages. Here it consists of attention to colour (orange, white, black), attractive font, and use of the 'heart' in the 'v'.

Folding leaflet (front and back)

Back cover uses same style but addresses the bully. This difference is shown by the heading, which isn't a question.

Helpline information given on back cover. Same colours as rest of leaflet but clearly set out for ease of reference.

Effective white, red and yellow cover, with clever image of broken heart/faces, to draw reader in.

If YOU are a BULLY.

Think about what you are doing to other people. Try and answer these questions:

- Why do you **BULLY** others?
- What do you get out of it?
- How do you think your victim feels?

If you are a **BULLY** and you want to stop, talk to someone. You can use the helplines on the back of this card.

Messages from people who have been **BULLIED:**

"You didn't just hurt me,
you hurt everyone who cares for me".

"You ruined my education".

"What did I ever do to you?"

Helpline Numbers for Information & Support
Bullying Online   www.bullying.co.uk
Childline *(freephone)*   0800 1111
Kidscape (and parent helpline)   0845 1205204
Anti-Bullying Campaign   0207 3781446
Parent Line   0808 800 222
Samaritans   0345 909 090
www.samaritans.org.uk
*(Listening service staffed 24hrs a day
every day of the year)*

Gloucestershire Youth & Community Service   01452 426391
Grapevine *(Young People's advice & information)* Cheltenham 01242 255888
                                   Gloucester   01452 500080
Astra Project   01452 541599
(alternative solutions to running away)
Share   01452 524019
(young people's counselling)

Oxford, Swindon & Gloucester

& THE FORESTERS' FUND
Produced by
The Park End Crew Youth Group
and Tuffley Street-Based Youth Workers.
Supported by
Gloucestershire Education Dept and Crimebeat

BULLYING RUINS LIVES

Information and Helplines for
Young People on **BULLYING**

Effective design: a lot of information packed into a small (105 X 75 mm) area when folded up.

Smaller text at foot of cover makes it clearer exactly what the leaflet is aiming to do.

Font for headings is clear but deliberately 'rough' to suggest harshness and urgency of the issue. Full caps used for effect.

Inside text starts with a definition of bullying.

Two types of **lists** are used:
• short paragraphs with first word in bold
• bullet lists.

Direct address used so that the leaflet is personal to the reader:
• pronoun 'you' used
• commands used.

What is BULLYING?

BULLYING is when somebody deliberately sets out to **hurt, threaten or frighten** someone.

BULLYING can be:

Physical - Tripping you up, throwing things at you, pulling your hair or hitting you.

Verbal - Name calling, racist remarks, persistent teasing.

Indirect - Spreading of nasty stories.

Why do people BULLY?

There are lots of reasons why people **BULLY**. Here are a few:

BULLIES may have been or are being bullied themselves.

- They might have trouble at home.
- They want to look **big** in front of others.
- They want to have power over you

Reasons for being BULLIED.

You can be **BULLIED** because you are **too fat**, or **too thin**. Because you **wear glasses**. Because of your **age, race, the way you talk, a disability**. Anyone could be **BULLIED**; there is **never** a **GOOD** reason for it. **It is not your fault.**

How can I stop people BULLYING me?

You **must** TELL someone you can trust:

- your **Mum, Dad or Grandparents**
- a **Friend**
- a **Teacher**
- a **Career or Youth Worker**

Keep a diary of what is happening to you. Practice what you are going to say either to an adult or the bully.

Don't give up. Tell, Tell, Tell!
Remember - You don't have to be a victim.

How can my school help?

Most schools will have rules on **BULLYING**. This is a plan that explains how to deal with **BULLIES**. Some schools have support groups for people who have been **BULLIED**. Find out about your school's policy.

How can my parents help?

Your Parents can visit your school and talk to your teachers. They or you can also get advice (and information booklets) from the **helpline numbers** on the back of this card.

What can you do to help someone who is being BULLIED?

Don't let people get **BULLIED** if you can help. If you think you can stop it try talking to both sides. **If that won't work, get some help from a teacher or parent.**

If you are friends with a BULLY, try talking to them to get them to stop.

Consistency of style throughout:
• headings (yellow) are questions
• main text is white
• 'bully' and 'bullied' always in full caps.

Straightforward language/style and short sentences used to communicate with all ages of young people.

Mixture of capitals and bold used to emphasise important words and phrases.

Advert

Prominent **text** ('copy') is straight and to the point. Implies a no-nonsense product. Appeals to audience (men).

'Short and sharp' is a **pun** – also refers to the effect of the gum.

Main image – handsome but not too trendy model. Implies:
• coolness with experience
• understated
• straight-talking (fits text).
Plays on audience's wish to look like/feel like this man.

Logo – as used on product.

Further copy to describe product. Note:
• short sentences for impact
• direct address
• pattern of positive + negative in first four lines
• some sentences are grammatically incomplete
• repetition of 'perfect' in last line.

slogan – its design reflects 'Extreme style' strip on product.

Image of **product**.

Visual impact is as important as the text. Note:
• 'clean cut' division of page into two columns
• dominance of image.
• use of black, white and blue
• text is **white on black** (WOB) – stylish impact, and again suitable for male audience.

Newspaper article

Catchy **headline** in full caps (all capital letters) draws reader in.

Popular papers pay more attention to **layout** and **visuals** than quality papers do.

Subhead underscored – tells you more about the story.

By-line gives reporter's name.

Opening paragraph sums up the story. Note bold font and first word in full caps.

Each paragraph is only one sentence (quality paper have slightly longer paragraphs).

Source of the article given a short way in – also explains why it is news (a new survey).

Eye-catching **subhead** – usually just a word or phrase from next section. Used to break up text.

More detail about the story given in **later paragraphs**.

Quotations from the report are in inverted commas.

Final paragraphs give further background to story, or widen the focus.

Caption to photo: note full caps and wordplay to draw you in.

DEATH OF THE LADETTE

Old-fashioned girls don't want to party

■ by LAURA NEILL

BRITISH women are rejecting the ladette lifestyle for an old-fashioned family role.

They're turning their backs on the hard-partying image made famous by the likes of Sarah Cox, 31, and Zoe Ball, 34.

Instead the so-called "new traditionalists" are married with children.

And they put the family before money and career, though they can combine both.

The new generation of 25 to 45-year-olds have been identified in a new survey.

They admire the values of their mother's era and believe in cooking and knitting, which has become trendy with the stars.

Twist

They snub food fads but know enough about health issues to realise what they should and shouldn't eat, according to the study for drinks firm Ovaltine.

Interviews with 500 women in the 25-45 age group found many wanted life to be "more like the old days" with a modern twist.

They believe in cooking meals for the family and not relying on fast food and dinner from a packet.

Instead of going out on the town, the new traditionalist prefers a "girls' night in".

A group of friends will gather at the home of one of their gang for a gossip.

Seven out of 10 women also thought life was probably better 50 years ago.

The emergence of the new traditionalist marks a swing away from the "having it all" breed to one who puts the family first, said the study.

Its findings illustrate

OUT OF DATE: Sara Cox, above, and, left, Ladette to Lady girls

KNIT WANTED: Girls would rather knit than be a ladette like Zoe Ball, above

Photo © Southern News & Pictures

Daily Star, 10 September 2005
copyright © Express Newspapers Ltd

Toolkits

Here are six 'toolkits' to help you remember the main features of the six communication types you have just looked at (pages 120–4).

Toolkit – Letters

Purpose – wide variety: information, persuasion, explanation, recount
Audience – businesses, friends and family
Structure and presentation
- writer's name and address at top right
- recipient's name and address at top left
- begin 'Dear …' and end 'Yours sincerely/faithfully' (if formal letter)
- formal letters make it clear at the start what they are about

Text
- style is clear and factual, if formal letter; standard English used
- informal letters include non-standard English and have a looser organisation

---

Toolkit – Leaflets

Purpose – to sell a product or give information or advice
Audience – anyone interested in the product or topic
Structure and presentation
- presentational devices are important
- bullet points, headings, etc. to break up text
- colours and font styles chosen to get message across

Text
- often short, snappy sentences to keep readers' attention
- direct address often used, to make leaflet personal to reader
- information leaflets aim for clear text; persuasive leaflets include rhetorical techniques
- sentences often not strictly grammatical

Toolkit – adverts

Purpose – to sell a product, or an idea (such as a political party, a campaign)
Audience – people who may buy that product
Structure and presentation
- design is key – it must attract the audience immediately
- image is usually more important than words
- logo, colours and font styles chosen to help sell product

Text
- slogan – memorable 'tag' to remind audience of product
- words often kept to a minimum, especially on display posters
- powerful and emotive words, for persuasive effect
- sentences often not strictly grammatical

Toolkit – newspaper stories

Purpose – to give information (especially quality papers), to entertain (especially popular papers)

Audience – people who read newspapers

Structure and presentation
- catchy headline draws reader in
- subheadings break up the text (especially popular papers)
- key points of story given first; more detail later; broader issues at end
- popular papers emphasise layout and photos; quality papers emphasise text

Text
- formal language and standard English used; popular papers can use less formal English
- often one sentence per paragraph; sentences shorter in popular papers
- if story is to inform, text is very clear; if it is to entertain, text is more descriptive
- key players or eyewitnesses are quoted; people's opinions are also quoted

Toolkit – Web pages

Purpose – wide variety, but especially persuasion (selling products) and information

Audience – anyone with access to a computer

Structure and presentation
- design is a feature of web pages – the page must attract the reader quickly
- structure of the page should be clear, to guide reader through all the text, images and interactivity
- links with other pages in the website, and with other websites, also important (hyperlinks)

Text
- style depends on the purpose and audience of the text
- text often not polished, as web designers have concentrated on design/ images
- successful web text makes its point quickly and powerfully, to keep reader's interest